Castalia, Ohio
44824
Phone-

WHEN DUST SHALL SING

BY GEORGE L. BRITT

WHEN DUST SHALL SING

THE WORLD CRISIS IN THE LIGHT
OF BIBLE PROPHECY

PATHWAY PRESS
Cleveland, Tennessee

WHEN DUST SHALL SING

Copyright, 1958, by Pathway Press
All rights reserved

No portion of this book may be used or reproduced in any manner, except in reviews and critical articles, without written permission from the publisher. Pathway Press, 922 Montgomery Avenue, Cleveland, Tennessee.

FIRST EDITION
SECOND PRINTING
THIRD PRINTING
FOURTH PRINTING

ISBN 0-87148-901-5

Library of Congress Catalog Card Number: 58-13663

Printed in the United States of America

With fervent gratitude to God for His gift of a beloved wife, two loving children and a happy home, this book is dedicated
to
My wife, Inez
My daughter, Norma Jean
My son, David Lee
with a prayer that because of the grace of Jesus Christ and consecration to God the family circle will be unbroken in eternity.

FOREWORD

It is the lot of this generation to live in momentous days. The simple way of life of our forefathers has been lost in a time of scientific advancement and technological invention. While the sciences of man have rushed forward, his morals have dropped ever farther behind. What the knowledge of our day has promised, its morals have not fulfilled. The result is confusion and uncertainty.

The advancement of knowledge and invention should have brought us a better day, but the lack of a corresponding moral and spiritual advancement conversely makes it a worse day, a day of evil potential, a day of threatening fear, a day of menace and moment. The Bible calls it "perilous times." It is indeed a time of peril when in one generation there is side by side such promise of good and such threat of evil. One wars against the other, and each for a time is frustrated by the other.

There is still another element that must be considered, an element that brings understanding instead of confusion. This is the design of God as it is revealed in His Word. Ignore this element and there is nothing but bewilderment and blindness; accept it and there is certainty and sense. What ignorant man sees as chance in his doings, enlightened man knows to be the working of God. It stands as absolute truth, then, that any effort to understand the momentous generation in which we live must begin with the Word of God.

An understanding of God's Word not only provides clarity for this day, but it casts its rays into the future so that we can see His design as it extends into tomorrow. This is one of the glories of God's relationship with His people.

The author of this book has distinguished himself for the past twenty-five years as a thorough scholar of the Scriptures. He has a rare and gifted insight into human experience and achievement as it relates to divine purpose. Few persons of today have such understanding of political science and public affairs as they unfold before the backdrop of Scripture. Coupled with his wisdom is his ability to convey his thoughts to others. This makes his book as interesting as it is important.

When Dust Shall Sing is a happy title. Strictly referring to the great resurrection of the righteous dead, it also has even greater and more immediate compass. Man's contrivances have brought the world to the brink of dust and ruin and chaos, but amid the shambles there is still hope and song for those who will believe. Author Britt leads us through the terrifying crises of our day, finding his way surely through the Word of God. The rise of communism, the apostate church, the turmoil of the Middle East, the spectre of nuclear destruction and other realities of our day are here, presented graphically and clearly. Yet amid the grimness there is hope, a Light, a song.

This is one of the finest books of prophetic studies I have ever had the pleasure of reading. It has the pulse of today's headlines and the anchor of the eternal Word.

Charles W. Conn

PREFACE

This book is the fruition of thirty years of studying and enjoying the Word of God. In this short space of time the writer has thrilled again and again as he beheld current events drop into their proper place in God's prophetic mold for history. He has seen it demonstrated in his lifetime that the Scriptures that tell of the future are just as authentic and immutable as those that relate the past.

An understanding of the prophetical Scriptures is not vital to one's salvation, but it does open such a vista of knowledge, hope, and joy that one who possesses it can live on a higher plane than one who does not. Such understanding is a great incentive to consecration. As a child of God beholds events occurring which were foretold thousands of years beforehand—and it is stated that these events will happen at the time of the end of this age—it causes him to see the vanity of this world in its true perspective and creates a desire for closer communion with God.

From time to time in over a quarter of a century of ministerial work, as I have given sermons and lectures on the divine prophecy in God's Word, I have had many requests for these lectures in writing. There has come a realization that many who believe in the Word have given too little time and prayerful study to the prophetical Scriptures to understand and enjoy them; nevertheless, they believe and rejoice in them.

This book is presented with the hope that it will stimulate a greater interest in the Scriptures which lead men to the path of light and eternal life, where we who see through a glass darkly now may see face to face, and we who know in part may know as we are known.

I wish to acknowledge gratefully the aid and encouragement which the Reverend Charles W. Conn has given me in the preparation of this material for the press. I also thank Mrs. C. E. French and Mrs. John Eubanks for their patience in copy-editing the material, and my daughter,

Norma Jean, for typing the original manuscripts.

I received inspiration from Dr. Louis S. Bauman's *Russian Events in the Light of Bible Prophecy,* Dr. C. I. Scofield's *Lectures on Prophecy* and F. J. Lee's *Book on Prophecy.* I also received aid from material from *Life* magazine, *Readers' Digest,* as well as news releases from the Associated Press and United Press and many other periodicals.

Greer, S. C. *George L. Britt*

TABLE OF CONTENTS

The Logic of Prophecy	15
The Wandering Jew Goes Home	27
New Life for Old Rome	39
The End of Russia	53
The Mystery of Babylon	69
The Miracle of The Jew	83
Times of the Gentiles	97
The Age of the Church	107
When Dust Shall Sing	139
When Men Seek Death	155
The Second Coming of Christ	175
The Mystery Kingdom	183
The Literal Kingdom of Heaven	191
A New Heaven and New Earth	199

WHEN DUST SHALL SING

INTRODUCTION

> *And at midnight there was a cry made, Behold, the bridegroom cometh; go ye out to meet him.—Matthew 25:6.*
>
> *For I delivered unto you first of all that which I also received, how that Christ died for our sins according to the scriptures; and that he was buried, and that he rose again the third day according to the scriptures.—1 Corinthians 15:3, 4.*

THE LOGIC OF PROPHECY

WE ARE now living in a time of the greatest moral decadence ever known to man. It is a time of world tension, bitter social strife, and phenomenal strides in science and physics; and the world is taut with a universal expectancy of still swifter and greater change. The last half century has witnessed a greater change in morals and a greater fulfillment of prophetical Scriptures than previous generations saw in fifteen hundred years. Building on the thought used by our Lord in His parable of the ten virgins in which He states that at midnight the cry was made, "Behold, the bridegroom cometh," and seeing the Scriptures concerning the end being so minutely fulfilled, and through scriptural enlightenment seeing the night shades of the great tribulation falling, we are persuaded to believe we are in the proximity of A.D.—11:30 p.m.

A New Age

Most prognosticators believe that we are on the threshold of a new age. Many tell us that the power of the atom will produce this new age. They believe the atom will drive our machines, do our housework, cure our ills, and produce synthetic food to feed earth's millions. Some think that some stillborn child of human futility, such as a world federation of nations, can bring in an age of perpetual peace. Still others profess to believe that man will bring an end to the world by a chain reaction of atomic fission or hydrogen fusion. Those who know God and His Word know we are on the brink of a new era and that the most momentous event of the entire age is imminent. They know this new age is very near and will be suddenly ushered in by the glorious appearing of the King of Kings and Lord of Lords. This is not just another man-conceived theory; if it were, it would be no more trustworthy than any of the other theories, but it is "according to the Scriptures." Paul made it clear to the Corinthians that all the gospel truths he preached and was willing to die for were according to the Scriptures.

If the United Nations should bring lasting peace and justice, it would not be according to the Scriptures. The Scriptures teach us that when man because of the result of his own efforts shall cry peace and safety, then sudden destruction shall come upon him (1

Thessalonians 5:3). Regardless of all man's moralizing and the prevalence of a self-helping social gospel this generation is gripped in vice, degeneracy, depravity, and crime. The Scriptures teach consistently that the age will grow worse and worse until it will end in catastrophe and the second coming of the Son of God. The Scriptures teach that perilous times will come and that the depraved race will give vent to their fallen nature (2 Timothy 3:1-3). The Scriptures teach that there will be a great falling away and the professing church will apostatize from the truth, having only a form (2 Thessalonians 2:3; Revelation 3:15, 16). The Scriptures also teach that they will be lovers of pleasure more than lovers of God (2 Timothy 3:4); selfishness, greed, vile affections, love of pleasure and vice are the hallmarks of this age. We can readily see that all the conditions of our age are according to the Scriptures.

It is useless for anyone to lose sleep for fear of the end of the age or world by atomic chain reaction; it would not tally with the Scriptures. It is amazing to hear well-known speakers, supposedly well-versed in the Scriptures, express this fear. God has let it be known how the age will end and it is not to end that way; so if man accidentally brings the end of the age by touching off a chain reaction, he will have changed God's Word and will. This is an impossible absurdity; it will end *according to the Scriptures.* This age will end in great tribulation (Matthew 24:21), and the kingdoms of this world will be ground into powder, but it will be brought about by the stone cut out of the mountain without hands (Daniel 2:34, 44), which is the second coming of the Son of God. There will be a complete change of the present world order which has already lost its equilibrium and is tottering (Daniel 2:35).

End of the Age

The tensions, perplexities and convulsions of our time are nothing more or less than the death throes of one age and the birth pangs of another. Many scoff at even the thought of the ending of this age. Mortal man without the inspiration of the Spirit and enlightenment of the Scriptures is incapable of rising to the pinnacle where he can get a true perspective of God's plan of the ages. Modern man with his tiny span of seventy or eighty years has never seen an age end, and being destitute of that faith which is the evidence of things not seen, he says this age will not end in the way the Scriptures teach—suddenly and supernaturally (Matthew 24:27; 1 Corinthians 15:51, 52).

This church age has already lasted nearly 2,000 years. All other ages have ended, why not this one? It was beyond the grasp of the antediluvians to believe Noah's message that their age would end, but their unbelief did not postpone the end one day when God's time arrived. Just so today carnal men cannot grasp the truth that the dispensation of the fullness of time (Ephesians 1:10) is dawning, that the immutable prophecies concerning the Davidic Covenant are nearing fulfillment, and that the literal kingdom of heaven is truly nigh at hand. Undoubtedly the current revival of preaching, proclaiming the nearness of the literal kingdom of heaven is the work of an all-wise God. When the King first appeared as Jesus of Nazareth, the Holy Spirit through John the Baptist, the Twelve, and also the Seventy, proclaimed that the kingdom of heaven was at hand. When the Jews rejected and slew the King, the resurrected King ascended to heaven as mediator of the new covenant. The Holy Spirit shifted the emphasis to the gospel of the grace of God that gives men power to become the sons of God and adopts them into the spiritual phase of the kingdom of heaven. Now that the time of the gentiles and the age of grace are ending, the Spirit of God is commingling the gospel of the grace of God with the gospel of the kingdom of heaven. Our present age which coincides with the mystery of the church age was hidden from past ages and in the plan of God is a parenthesis between the first advent and the second advent which will usher in the literal kingdom of heaven. This parenthesis or mystery of the church has not abrogated one prophecy concerning the literal kingdom of heaven, which will be fulfilled every jot and tittle according to the Scriptures.

Jesus' references to the end of this age are too numerous to mention here. He was so specific about the end of this age that He gave signs whereby we could know when it is near, even at the door. He did not hedge or confuse with vague generalities in His teaching about the end of this age, but was plain and specific. Jesus, as well as the apostles, held out the truth that this age will end as one of the greatest incentives for His followers to watch, purify themselves and be true to the faith.

The Secrets of God

Blessed is the child of God who can soar by faith above the limited perspective of ordinary men to the mountaintop of prophetic Scripture, and thrill to the panorama of fulfilled prophecy being unfolded by the hand of an omnipotent God. When a child of God by simple, sincere faith in the Scriptures soars to this elevation, he reaches the plane where the tangible, tawdry, glittering things of this life have lost their appeal; and he has no need for the superficial and sensational to bolster his faith, but can thrill with inward exaltation that the omniscient One has confided in him. It is pathetic today to see so many who profess a deep experience appealing to that which is shallow and superficial. So many are seeking cheap sensationalism when they could drink deep at the well of eternal truth and experience the thrill of real intimacy with God. It is a mark of real spirituality to be able to behold the fulfillment of prophecy and rejoice in what God is doing. Prophecy is one of the most beneficent blessings and favors of God to mankind. It even shows the extent of God's love and blessings to His redeemed; it brings the redeemed into a special intimacy with God.

Dr. C. I. Scofield expresses it eloquently in his *Lectures on Prophecy:* "I say, it is the study of the prophetic truths; the receiving from God of the revelations concerning His future purposes in that which concerns us and the world, that brings us into a peculiar intimacy with God Himself. Christ says, 'I have called you friends; I have not called you servants.' What is the difference? What is the proof He gives of having placed us in the relationship of friend? This: 'For all things that I have heard of my Father, I have made known unto you.' Friendship is an intimate relation, you see, and involves confidences. Abraham was called the friend of God, and the Lord said: 'Shall I hide from Abraham that which I do?' Now when God gives a prophecy He takes us into a wonderful personal intimacy. Let us, then, accept God's invitation to come unto these, His deepest counsels, to sit with Him in heavenly places while He unfolds to us the great secret of His majestic and amazing purposes. If we are ready to admit that there is a mighty influence in association, in intimacy, if we feel its effect in the human relationship in which we stand, need I argue for one moment that that part of the divine truth which brings us into the most intimate fellowship with Jehovah Himself must have the mightiest influence upon our character, and so ultimately upon our conduct?

"I confess with shame that there was a time in my Christian life when I thought lightly of prophecy;

when I said to myself, if not in words, at least in fact, 'What has that to do with me? What I wish to know is how I may be saved, how I may get blessings, how I may get to heaven. Never mind what God intends to do with the Jewish people; never mind what His purposes are toward the world; He will in due time fulfill all these things. Why should I care particularly what He is going to do with Israel? I am not an Israelite.' I say there was a time when that was my attitude toward the prophecies. Do you not see that I was actually refusing the most intimate fellowship with the Lord?"

When the former things are passed away (Revelation 21:4) and man's probation is over; when *finis* is written to time, and the standards of time are replaced by those of eternity, then shall it be revealed that the wise of the race of men were not those who majored in the laws God gave to govern matter, or in the fields of human endeavor, but those who majored in fellowship with the Omnipotent One, of whom it is written, "Known unto God are all of His works from the beginning of the world."

Grace Was Once Prophecy

This glorious grace we enjoy today was for centuries known only by prophecy. Every sermon preached today about this grace is preached about a subject that for centuries was prophecy. Do those who dismiss prophecy with a shrug mean that they despise unfulfilled prophecy and love fulfilled prophecy? Peter in his great sermon on the Day of Pentecost adhered to the same rule as Paul, and appealed to the prophecies in the Scriptures. He cited his hearers to the prophecies in Joel, and affirmed that the wonderful events that happened that day were all "according to the Scriptures."

We have known in time past some who minimized the urgent need of studying the Word, because, as they said, they had the Spirit to teach them. In due time their Christian experience consisted of feelings alone and when sudden temptation came they yielded easily. They had failed to grow strong because one can grow only by the sincere milk of the Word.

It is true that an understandable knowledge of the grace of God is sufficient to be saved, but it is also true that it is a mark of depth and Christian maturity to be able to rejoice in the future as unfolded by prophecy. Hope ranks with faith and love in that tripartite foundation on which Christian growth and character are built. Hope maketh not ashamed, but rather gives us boldness (Romans 5:5). Hope, the anchor of the soul, sustains, thrills, and beacons amidst all the vagaries of life (Hebrews 6:19). Hope causes purification as nothing else will (1 John 3:3). How is this precious possession obtained? It is begotten and nourished by the sure word of prophecy.

When the Son of God came into this world by the way of Bethlehem, He fulfilled such a multitudinous array of specific prophecies that it was a mathematical impossibility for an imposter to take His place. Jesus said He came to fulfill the prophets (Matthew 5:17). When He stood up in the synagogue at Nazareth and read the prophecies in Isaiah concerning Himself— prophecy uttered 725 years before that time—He said, "This day is this scripture fulfilled." Christ was conscious of the fact that every act of His life was fulfilling prophecy.

Christ was born of a virgin to fulfill the prophecy of Isaiah 7:14; of the family of David to fulfill Psalm 89:3, 4 and Isaiah 11:1. Herod slew the innocents to fulfill Jeremiah 31:15; Joseph fled from Herod's wrath and went into Egypt to fulfill, "Out of Egypt have I called my Son" (Hosea 11:1). He was not crucified alone but between two thieves to fulfill, "He was numbered with the transgressors" (Isaiah 53:12). The soldiers did not just happen to gamble for His garments, but it was to fulfill, "They part my garment among them, and cast lots upon my vesture" (Psalm 22:18). They omitted the custom of their day and did not break His legs that prophecy might be fulfilled (Numbers 9:12; John 19:31-37). Divine providence provided the colt at the right place at the right time, that it might be fulfilled, "Thy King cometh unto thee: he is just, and having salvation; lowly, and riding upon an ass, and upon a colt the foal of an ass" (Zechariah 9:9). It was just mentioned one time in prophecy that Christ would be born in Bethlehem, but the whole world was shuffled and moved that it might happen according to the Scriptures.

INTRODUCTION

How can an enlightened child of God keep from being thrilled by current events that tell us plainly that Christ's second coming is near according to the Scriptures. Why should it be counted a thing incredible to a true Christian that God should know the future? He named Cyrus over a century before he was born and then used him to fulfill prophecy and to give the decree that Israel should return. When God gave the prophecy that proud Tyre, the mistress of the sea, would be destroyed and the very stones, timbers and dust of the city would be cast into the midst of the water, it seemed to men of that day as unlikely to happen as the end of the age does to men today. Yet, God used two world empires to fulfill this one prophecy. God used Nebuchadnezzar of the Babylonian Empire to fulfill part of this prophecy when he destroyed the old city of Tyre, but the prophecy that stated the very dust would be laid in the midst of the water was not fulfilled. One jot or tittle of God's immutable Word cannot fail without fulfillment. So young Prince Alexander, of Macedonia, became obsessed with a desire to march eastward and conquer. The men of Macedonia and of all Greece began to mobilize from the hills and valleys to march on a long journey to fulfill one sentence in prophecy. When they arrived at faraway Tyre the people of Tyre had built their new city on an island out in the sea. The soldiers of Alexander set to work and with ardent perseverence laid the timbers, stones and dust of the old city in the sea to build a causeway to the new city and capture it. Thus after two hundred and fifty years the men of Greece marched long and far and fulfilled completely Ezekiel 26:12.

If students of prophecy try to match wits or put on an exhibition of personal wisdom or become too dogmatic in details, such as naming the antichrist, they may unconsciously lend themselves to Satan's efforts to stigmatize prophetical teaching. We may never know all the details of the immediate future, but God wills that we have, and we can have, a clear general outline of the events immediately preceding the end of this age, and we can have enough details to know when it is near, even at the door.

We find in the prophetical Scriptures certain specific world conditions that are to exist at the end of this age that did not exist fifteen years ago, but do exist today. At least if they existed at all they were in an embryonic state, and were not as clear and tangible as today.

The same omnipotent God that gave the laws that the solar system so meticulously obeys, gave the prophecies in His Word. As surely as seedtime and harvest, day and night, winter and summer have to obey God's decree (Genesis 8:22), just that surely these prophecies will be fulfilled according to the Scriptures.

CHAPTER 1

THE WANDERING JEW GOES HOME

> *And it shall come to pass in that day, that the Lord shall set his hand again the second time to recover the remnant of his people, which shall be left, from Assyria, and from Egypt, and from Pathros, and from Cush, and from Elam, and from Shinar, and from Hamath, and from the islands of the sea.—Isaiah 11:11.*
>
> *Therefore prophesy and say unto them, Thus saith the Lord God; Behold, O my people, I will open your graves, and cause you to come up out of your graves, and bring you into the land of Israel.—Ezekiel 37:12.*

HIS aged heart pounded laboriously that hot summer day of 1948. Hot tears of joy trickled down the leathery face wrinkled by ninety years of life lived under the torrid sun of Yemen. The deep-set eyes in the mummylike face showed emotions too deep for the tongue to express. These emotions were wrung from a human heart by the climactic end of ninety years of faith and hope. The object of his faith lay there beneath the wings of the large four-motored plane. Now, at last, his long-cherished hope had ended in sight. As the plane reduced its speed and began to circle for a landing this son of Abraham strained with eagerness to see more of the land promised Abraham and his seed 3,870 years before that particular summer day. The shadow of the plane glided swiftly and silently over the same terrain touched by the feet of Jonah as he tried to flee from the Lord. The plane landed at the airport of Tel Aviv, the city built in 1909, just three miles north of the same spot on which Joppa stood. This modern commercial city, however, was 2,800 years removed from the Joppa of Jonah's day.

As the plane taxied to a stop, young excited Jews pressed toward the exit of the plane, forcing the aged Jew and his son of threescore years to be the last passengers to depart. The old man was rendered immobile by the deep emotions surging in his breast, plus his great age. It was so difficult for him to realize, yet it was true, that he was seeing what many prophets had foretold, had believed, and had hoped to see, but had died without seeing. His ancestors for 1,900 years had lived as aliens in the hot, dry country of Yemen. They had carefully copied and preserved the scrolls containing the promises of God that He would regather Israel. The sixty-year-old son carried his frail father pickaback fashion off the plane. When the old man's feet touched the soil promised to Abraham and his seed, he fell prostrate, convulsed with deep emotions. He grasped handfuls of soil, kissed it and cried, "God has kept His promises to Israel."

The pilots of the planes and the sailors of the ships that were bringing Jews from almost every country in the world to Tel Aviv and Haifa, were unaware that they had a rendezvous with destiny. God was permitting them to participate in the most momentous event in 2,000 years. God was fulfilling His promises made through the prophets to Israel and the world that He would regather Israel. Not all of the seed of Abraham was returning at this time, but a remnant had returned and had hoisted the star of David above the soil of Palestine. After nearly 2,000 years of dispersion there was an Israel again in the economy of nations.

This momentous event failed to have the impact upon this money-mad, pleasure-mad generation that students of prophecy thought that it would have when it came to pass. They hardly paused for comment from their eating, drinking, buying and selling, marrying and giving in marriage. They are blind to the fact that this event ushered in the beginning of the end of the "times of the Gentiles" (Luke 21:24). Many people shrugged it off as just another readjustment caused by World War II; but in the plan of Him whose kingdom rules over all, it was one of the main causes of World War II. The war shuffled world conditions into a favorable position for the end of the age. Russia emerged from the war strong enough to fulfill her role foretold in Ezekiel 38, 39. This war broke down the nationalistic barriers in Europe so the ten-nation union foretold in prophecy could form. The atrocities committed during the war shocked world Jewry into fulfilling God's will by giving them a fanatical desire for a national home.

This is an example of how the omnipotent God can make all things work according to His will. For nearly 1,900 years they were complacent in their adopted countries. When God's clock of prophecy ticked to the predestined hour, Hitler and the war quickly changed this complacency into desperation. They crowded every old ship they could buy to the utmost capacity and flocked to the Promised Land. When the English navy stopped them at the three-mile limit many leaped into the sea and tried to swim ashore. For many centuries while God's sentence of dispersion was upon them there was no incentive for them to go back. Now that the "times of the Gentiles" was nearing the end and the time for the Scriptures to be fulfilled had arrived, God made the Promised Land as alluring to thousands of them as it was to their forefathers who had followed Moses out of Egypt.

The aforesaid old man, who kissed the soil of Israel, had, according to God's promise, been brought up from the Jewish "grave" in Yemen. At first, the Zionist leaders did not believe that there was a group of exiled Jews who had been buried from sight on the southern extremity of the Arabian peninsula. Investigation proved that they were full-blooded Jews who had kept the scrolls of the Hebrew Scriptures zealously for centuries.

THE WANDERING JEW GOES HOME

The Jew is one of God's greatest miracles. Although "buried" among the nations for almost two millenniums, the nations have not been able to digest or assimilate them. Without a national home and without a ruler, they have been banished from country after country—disfranchized, segregated in ghettos, hounded, persecuted, and slain. They have wandered from country to country, from continent to continent, yet they are a full-blooded, distinct race, a most peculiar people. Without the direct providence of God, they would have lost their identity in the stream of humanity. God has reserved for them in the near future their greatest glory. One of the most prominent prophetical assurances in God's Word is the assurance that when the "times of the Gentiles" has come to an end and the fullness of the gentiles be come in (Romans 11:25), Israel's dispersion will end and they will be gathered to their homeland. The Davidic Covenant will be fulfilled (2 Samuel 7:16; Luke 1:32) and for 1,000 years, during the literal kingdom of heaven that they have looked for so long, they will see their greatest glory.

The "times of the Gentiles" began in 606 B.C. when the Jews went into captivity into Babylon, and will end when Christ, at His second coming, crushes the Antichrist and his ten-nation confederacy (Daniel 2:44; Revelation 19:19-21).

The fullness of the gentiles began with the gospel age when salvation by faith was offered to the gentiles. During the gospel age, God has gathered from the gentiles a people for His name. The fullness of the gentiles will end when those in Christ are raptured, at least seven years before the "times of the Gentiles" ends. According to the Scriptures, there has to be a Jewish nation back in the homeland besieged by at least ten gentile nations when the "times of the Gentiles" ends (Z e c h a r i a h 14:2, 3; Revelation 17:12-14).

The regathering of Israel, the second coming of Christ, and the rapture of the saints are closely connected chronologically. It is an admitted fact that they are not all back and those that are, are still unconverted, but there is a remnant back home and the world beholds a self-governed Israel in the homeland after 2,000 years in exile.

The hands on God's world clock are nearing a momentous hour. Some of the most reiterated promises in God's Word are that Israel will be gathered back to the homeland. It would become monotonous and consume too much space to give all of the Scriptures referring to the regathering of Israel. The following are sufficient to prove that their return is not an accident of history, but the fulfillment of the Scriptures: "Therefore, behold, the days come, saith the Lord, that it shall no more be said, The Lord liveth, that brought up the children of Israel out of the land of Egypt; but, The Lord liveth, that brought up the children of Israel from the land of the north, and from all the lands whither he hath driven them: and I will bring them again into their land that I gave unto their fathers," Jeremiah 16:14, 15.

"Fear not: for I am with thee: I will bring thy seed from the east, and gather thee from the west; I will say to the north, Give up; and to the south, Keep not back: bring my sons from far, and my daughters from the ends of the earth," Isaiah 43:5, 6.*

A most significant fact to us today is that almost without exception the Scriptures connect the regathering of Israel with the second coming of the Son of God and the beginning of the kingdom age. For instance, Zephaniah 3:20 reads, "At that time will I bring you again, even in the time that I gather you." What is meant by *at that time*? The preceding verses 8-20 have just described the glories of the kingdom when the Lord will be in the midst of Israel. A pure language shall be given to the people that they shall serve the Lord with one consent, and Israel shall not see evil any more. This can mean nothing but the kingdom age. At *that time*—near the beginning of the kingdom age—Israel shall be regathered. Again in Micah 4:6, we read: "In that day, saith the Lord, will I assemble her that halteth, and I will gather her that is driven out, and her that I have afflicted." The *that day* here means the same as in all kindred passages. The five preceding verses of this chapter tell how the mountain of the house of the Lord shall

---
* Those interested in further references should also note Deuteronomy 30:3-5; Jeremiah 23:3, 7, 8; 29:14; 30:10; 31:8-10; Ezekiel 11:17; 20:34; 28:25; 37:21; Isaiah 54:7-10; Zechariah 10:9, 10; Micah 2:12; Romans 11:25. In fact, there are more Scriptures stating directly that Israel will be regathered than there are stating directly the first advent of Jesus.

be established, the Lord shall judge among many nations, they shall beat their swords into plowshares, their spears into pruninghooks, nation shall not lift up a sword against nation, neither shall they learn war any more. Every Bible student knows that this describes the beginning of the millennial reign. The Scriptures state that in *that day* (near the beginning of the millennium) Israel will be regathered. So is the trend throughout prophecy—the regathering of Israel is connected with the soon coming of the Lord to begin the literal kingdom of heaven.

In the books of Daniel and Revelation God reveals much of the last seven years of Israel's history before the promised kingdom begins. Israel has to be back in the land as an autonomous nation before the events of this week of years can transpire. Daniel learned from Jeremiah 25:11, 12 that seventy years were determined for the Jews to be in captivity in Babylon. While Daniel was praying for God to hasten the day, God revealed something of far greater importance than the seventy years. God revealed that seventy weeks were determined for Israel to be under gentile domination before the kingdom blessings could come in (Daniel 9:24-27). History and the fulfillment of prophecy have proved these weeks to be weeks of years. These weeks were divided into three divisions: seven weeks, sixty-two weeks, and one week. These weeks were to begin at the going forth to restore and to build Jerusalem, which was 445 B.C., when Nehemiah returned by permission of Artaxerxes (Nehemiah 2:6). Satan has tried to stigmatize prophetical Scriptures by causing men to set dates. Here God sets dates and when God does it, history authenticates the dates. In seven weeks, plus sixty-two weeks, the Messiah was to come and be cut off (crucified). Seven plus sixty-two equals sixty-nine weeks. Seven years times sixty-nine years equals 483 years. Therefore, God's prophetical Scripture states that Christ would be crucified 483 years from the time Nehemiah began to build. From 445 B.C. to A.D. 30, the year Christ was crucified, is only 475 years; therefore, many have thought they have found a discrepancy in the Bible. When we substitute the scriptural year of 360 days for the astronomical year of 365¼ days, we have the 483 years. Here again the Scriptures stand immutable. Christ came and was crucified the very year it had been foretold that it would occur.

Hidden from the Old Testament prophets in the councils of God was the mystery of the church, the age which has filled the 1,900 years' parenthesis between the sixty-ninth and seventieth weeks. God ceased to deal with Israel as a nation in their own land when they rejected and crucified their King. They were broken off for a time that the gentiles might be grafted in by faith (Romans 11:17-20). During this parenthesis between the sixty-ninth and seventieth weeks the gentiles have been the recipients of God's grace. Yet there remains hanging in suspension, as it were, the seventieth week of Israel's history. This is destined to be earth's most momentous week until she is worked over by fire. More world-shaking events will be crowded into this seven years than into any century of man's existence.

This week of seven years is destined to finish the transgression, to make an end of sins, to make reconciliation for iniquity, to bring in everlasting righteousness, to seal up the vision and prophecy, and to anoint the Most Holy. This week is so world-shaking that God takes fourteen chapters of the book of Revelation to describe it (Revelation 6:1-19:21).

This week is known in Scripture as the time of Jacob's trouble (Jeremiah 30:7), and also as the great tribulation (Matthew 24:21; Revelation 7:14). Christ, referring to the last half of this week, said there never has been a time like it and never shall be again. At the beginning of this week Israel will confirm a covenant with the Antichrist, the ruler of the ten confederated nations within the territory of the old Roman Empire. When their King came to Israel they rejected Him and crucified Him. Christ, referring to this covenant with the Antichrist, says, "I am come in my Father's name and ye receive me not: if another shall come in his own name, him ye will receive" (John 5:43). In the middle of the week the Antichrist will break his covenant (Daniel 9:27). At this time the Jews will experience the most intense agony of their agony-filled history. This week just ahead is the darkest hour—just before the dawn of the glorious kingdom they have hoped for so long, when Christ will sit on the throne at Jerusalem and the knowledge of the Lord will cover the earth like the waters cover the sea (Isaiah 11:9).

Because of the synchronizing of current events with so many of the prophetical Scriptures, surely the "time of the Gentiles" is near an end and God is ready to take up the thread of Israel's history and fulfill the last week before the kingdom blessings begin. It is true that there are only 1.6 million Jews back in Israel now, but they are returning at a fast rate. In 1949, 243,500 returned; in 1951, 175,000 returned; and also the United Jewish Appeal financed the return of an estimated 110,000 in 1957. A corresponding number have returned in the intervening years. In 1950 Israel brought back by air transport 50,000 Jews from Iraq alone. It is hardly conceivable, and difficult to prove scriptural, that all Jews will ever be back in Israel. The startling fact is that there is an Israel among the nations for the first time since A.D. 70. The stage is set for the last act in the drama of this age. The last pieces of the jigsaw puzzle of prophecy are being pushed into place by an omnipotent hand.

Another fact worthy of note is that a great pinnacle or crisis has been reached in human history approximately every 2,000 years. When we consider the five and one-fourth days lost by reckoning time by the astronomical year rather than the scriptural year, we find that we are much nearer the end of the 2,000 years since Christ than 1958 indicates.

If we wish to disregard all types, we still have the fulfillment of the more sure word of prophecy (2 Peter 1:19) that lets us know that the end of this age is near. It is hard for the finite mind to grasp the fact that this generation is witnessing the dying throes of an age. Prophets foretold it, apostles wrote about it, martyrs died believing it would come, generations of preachers have preached about it, Christians for ages have sung about it, and from all the evidence of fulfilled Scripture this generation will see it. The wisest people on earth today are those that are consecrated to Jesus Christ and ready for the rapture.

CHAPTER II

NEW LIFE FOR OLD ROME

> *And in the days of these kings shall the God of heaven set up a kingdom, which shall never be destroyed: and the kingdom shall not be left to other people, but it shall break in pieces and consume all these kingdoms, and it shall stand for ever.*—Daniel 2:44.

I WISH to relate two events that clearly depict the dangerous spirit and philosophy that has our generation in a death grip. I have before me an article from the daily press entitled "Heaven's View Is Perceptive." The article represents the conclusions of a symposium composed of ministers of various faiths in which they advocate the theory that heaven's view is deceptive. They presume that all intelligent clergymen disbelieve that heaven is real and that those who taught it was real in time past "thought in simpler terms." They go so far as to say, "The infiltration of pagan notions caused some past efforts to make the abstract into the concrete, the spiritual into the corporeal, the sublime into the tangible." They conclude with one accord that heaven is only a symbol.

In regard to this, may I ask, could it be a mark of intelligence to believe that hundreds of thousands of martyrs willingly were skinned alive, sawn asunder, and burned at the stake because they believed these excruciating deaths would give them a passport into a symbol? Is it intelligent to believe that the astute reasoner Paul was in a strait betwixt two when he tried to decide whether he would rather live in this world or depart to be with a symbol? Could it be possible that a view of this symbol was so breathtaking, so awe-inspiring, so exalting, that the greatest preacher that ever lived had to carry a thorn in the flesh to keep him humble because he had the one peek at this symbol?

Satan, from his pinnacle of power as the god of this world and author of the world systems, has been very successful in his efforts to delude men into believing that the glorious promises of God and personal salvation for men are only myths and symbols. He has infiltrated the pulpits and colleges, including theological schools, with the poison of scepticism. He has saturated our generation with the idea that the Bible is fallible, a product of man; that the truths of the Bible are fables, heaven is a symbol, miracles are a fallacy, the devil is an invention, hell is a myth, God is an abstraction, and prophecy is a fabrication.

We see it demonstrated in this world every day that pain is real, sorrow is real, disease is real, poverty is real, and death is real. Those of this present age who do not know that God is real, that fellowship with Him is real, that salvation, hope, and our eternal destination are real are of all men most miserable. It is pathetic to see Satan's success in making men believe that religion is a vague mysticism and if man wants his desires satisfied, his joy increased, and his emotions stirred, he will have to turn to sin and Satan's system. Satan does not care how many times we join a church or how much ritualism we endure so long as we never let our longings be for fellowship with God, never let His Word be our desire, never let our meditations be on God, never let His presence thrill us or His promise fortify our hope until it is the anchor of our soul. Satan says never get excited over religion, serve God in a sedate, shallow ritual, but when it comes to our emotions and hearts, give them all to him. Satan, controlling as he does the propaganda and entertainment media, makes men believe that the only real things are earth's tangibles, such as gold, shiny limousines, spacious mansions, nicotine, alcohol, and especially sex. By all means he does not want men to believe that the promises in prophecy are real and imminent.

The other incident to which I wish to refer concerns a minister who, when he learned that the members of his church were interested in the book of Daniel and were listening to lectures on this book, became disturbed and abusive and told his members that the book of Daniel did not mean anything. Surely he did not realize the seriousness of his statement, because he professed to believe that the Gospels do mean something. The Son of God of the Gospels affirmed the authenticity of Daniel by referring to a portion of the book and incorporating it into His discourse on the end of the age (Matthew 24:15-18). If Daniel is a myth, then where does this place the Son of God? The fact is that many modern atheists use this same line of logic to try to strip Christ of His deity. They say that Christ believed and taught many of the myths and errors of His day and, therefore, was limited in knowledge as other men of His time; that He was only a good moral teacher.

God gave His promises in prophecy for the edification and joy of His children and to nurture their hope. It pleases God for us to be enthralled with His promises. To Daniel was revealed more of the future than to any other man with the possible exception of John. This whetted his appetite to such an extent that he wanted to know more (Daniel 12:8). We see God's attitude toward Daniel's desire to know more when the angel stated, "Thou art greatly beloved."

When the greatest event of all the ages happened, the studious scribes, the learned rabbis, and the sanctimonious priests were unaware that it was even near. The intelligentsia of the Jewish nation were oblivious to the fact that the most outstanding event of all the ages had occurred. Even the astute, brilliant Saul of Tarsus was in darkness and could not discern the

NEW LIFE FOR OLD ROME 43

signs of the times. It was unpretentious, insignificant Anna and Simeon who had living, implicit faith in the prophetic Scriptures and who possessed wisdom not of this world, who thrust their heads above the foul atmosphere of their day, polluted with religious bigotry, hypocrisy, and self-righteousness, and breathed the pure, clean air of divine revelation, while the great in this world's wisdom milled around and around in their little world of self-conceit. As it was then, so it is today.

There are gleams of prophetic truth in almost all the books of the Bible, but some (such as Daniel and Revelation, which are almost exclusively prophetical in content) deal more with future events than others. In the book of Daniel God uses visual aid to simplify and aid us in understanding world history in advance. He uses the image of a man in Daniel 2 to depict the future history of the world. He begins with the head of gold and explains that it represents Babylon, the empire in existence at the time the vision was given. He progresses with the consecutive world empires down to the toes, where He reveals that in the time of the toes organized human government will be ended by the second coming of the Son of God and God will set up the kingdom of heaven, a theocracy on earth. In the seventh chapter of Daniel God gives a vision of four beasts, which covers the same period of time and represents the same world governments as Daniel 2. In chapter seven God revealed a detail not given in chapter two—that the ten-nation union within the territory of the old Roman Empire at the time the God of heaven sets up His kingdom will be ruled over by the little horn, the man of sin, the beast (Daniel 7:24-27). In Revelation 17, where the sharing of power between the Antichrist's government and the world powerful apostate church is shown by the symbols of the ten-horned beast and the scarlet woman, God reaffirms that ten nations within the geographical territory of the Roman Empire will be in a federation at the time of the end.

Many adults today with a rural background can recall pleasant scenes of childhood, when freshly churned butter was pressed into hand molds intricately carved with floral designs. When the butter was released from the mold, it bore the exact image of the mold. Those who have seen an iron foundry in operation have seen how the molten iron is cast into sand molds; when the iron cools it bears the exact image of the mold. The omnipotent God, who is the Architect and Executor of the ages, gave a mold in the book of Daniel for world history to be poured into. Revealed future world events as in Daniel are known as prophecy. Recorded past world events are known as history. As time transpired and world events were pressed into every crevice of this prophetic mold, they came out as world history. This history bears the exact image of the mold.

This is the one truth that the sceptics, atheists, and agnostics fear to tackle. With a flamboyant air they will wave Darwin's *Origin of Species,* and declare it supercedes Moses' *Genesis.* With blatant boldness they will try to take away the glorious wisdom of our Creator exhibited in His wonderful variations in nature, and contribute it to the power of mutation possessed by the microscopic gene. They dismiss miracles with a wave of the hand, and do not hesitate to commit blasphemy in explaining away the virgin birth. When it comes to explaining how a young Hebrew captive in a foreign land could take his pen and write a detailed history of the world for thousands of years in advance, all those sceptics who make any pretence of honesty and objectivity are conspicuously silent. This is the one revelation of God's omnipotence that puny human reasoning cannot becloud in the pretence of seeking truth, without betraying dishonesty and insincerity. They cannot deny that history has been poured into the prophetic mold without exposing their dishonesty. On the other hand, if in their desperation to do away with the real God they attribute to a mere man the power to know and order the future, then they create themselves a god. The reason for the silence of the loquacious sceptics on this subject is very obvious. Yet some ministers will speak disparingly about this same book of Daniel that sceptics fear most.

God in His preview of history before it occurred even gave the unusual characteristic of the power that would succeed Babylon, that it would consist of a union of two nations under one crown. We all know how history poured the two nations Media and Persia into the prophetic mold to cast the arms and breast of the image of Daniel 2.

Why do not the higher critics in their pretence of honest objectivity explain this one? How could a mere man, amusing himself by fabricating a myth, look into the future and tell in detail the name of the nation that would overthrow Medo-Persia and give the minute facts that at the height of his glory the heroic commander of Greece would be broken off, or die, and that four of his generals would divide his empire? In their forced silence the critics unwillingly proclaim the omniscience of our glorious Creator and the immutability of His Word. Even the lowly microbe that caused the death of Alexander stepped in and played its part in casting history according to the prophetic mold. God did not stop with a general outline of future world history, but He went into a detailed outline of the fortune and wars of two of these kingdoms yet to come; namely, Syria and Egypt (Daniel 8:7-14; 11:4-35). It seems obvious that God gave detailed attention to one of these lesser kingdoms in order to give the background and origin of a notorious personage, who would play such an important part in the fulfillment of so many prophecies dealing with the last days.

According to the divine mold for history, the fourth world empire—the one succeeding Greece— would be mightier, stronger and more terrible than any of the others. God also revealed that this would

NEW LIFE FOR OLD ROME 47

be the last world empire and that it would break up into autonomous nations represented by the toes of the image. God also revealed in the Scripture something else of importance—that in the end of the age this empire would exist for a very short time by a reunion of these toe nations (Daniel 7:7; Revelation 13:5; 17:12, 13).

To men of Daniel's day, living during the glory of Babylon, with her magnificent hanging gardens and all of her pomp and power, to hear that there would arise an empire that would dwarf the glories of Babylon must have staggered their faith. When God's time arrived, out stepped the fourth world empire, Rome, and fulfilled God's Word in every detail. How little did the small band of Latins who pitched their camp on the Palatine Hill, situated on the banks of the Tiber River in central Italy about 750 B.C., realize that this little village was the beginning of the greatest and strongest world empire ever to exist until the time of the end! Just so today, how little do men realize that history is being made according to the divine mold and cannot be molded otherwise.

About A.D. 476, just as the Scriptures foretold, this greatest of empires crumbled into the toes of Daniel's image, which are the modern nations of today within the territory of the Roman Empire. According to man's view, or profane history, the Roman Empire has not existed for many centuries. It is true that the emperors ceased to be and Imperial

Rome faded away, but as she faded she blended into the ecclesiastical Roman Empire and a mighty pontiff stepped on the throne of the Caesars. Through this ecclesiastical empire the power of Rome has never ceased to influence world affairs. For many centuries this pontiff ruled many nations supremely in political affairs as well as ecclesiastical affairs, and even today this successor to the Caesars rules over nearly 500,000,000 people. The toe kingdoms govern themselves largely by Roman law even today and many speak a form of Latin.

The Scriptures that tell us that the nations in the territory of the Roman Empire will be united in a confederacy in the last days do not recognize this confederacy as another empire, but the last stage of the Roman Empire. The Scriptures also reveal that this federation governed by the little horn (Daniel 7:8), the Beast (Revelation 13:1-8), the man of sin (2 Thessalonians 2:3, 4), the Antichrist (1 John 4:3) will continue only a short time (Revelation 13:5; 17:10). His rule will be shortened by the coming of the Son of God, who will smite his armies and cast him into the lake of fire. If all the centuries of human history from Babylon down to now have been molded according to the foreview in Daniel, how can anyone doubt that the remaining years of this age will be cast according to the mold?

Many ambitious, proud conquerors have tried to carve out world empires contrary to this Scriptural mold, but have failed. It seemed at times that they would succeed, but they could not with their mighty armies change one sentence of Scripture. It seemed that Napoleon at one time would establish his empire, but he met his Waterloo. The Kaiser of World War I had ambitions that were not according to the Scriptures, but he met his Verdun. Then when Adolf Hitler was in a handbreadth of succeeding, with Poland, Holland, Belgium, France, Norway, and Luxemburg under his heel, Italy, Austria, Hungary, and Bulgaria fighting at his side, and England lying prostrate before him across the narrow English Channel, he did that which can never be understood except by believers in prophecy—he turned his back on victory, marched east and met his Stalingrad. Gog, with his legions of Magog, has had ambitions of world dominion and is preparing to march, but he is certain to meet his Hamon-gog when he attacks Israel (Ezekiel 39:11).

The nations have been in the toe stage of Daniel's image for centuries with the status quo only occasionally being disturbed by localized wars. Just as the immutable prophecies foretold that they would not cleave together, they have been fanatically nationalistic. They have had their separate governments, trade barriers, currencies, and armies, and for over one thousand years have gone their own separate ways.

Today something is happening in these toe nations. They are in a state of agitation and change. The one-world doctrine has become popular. The doctrine of internationalism is openly advocated by some United States senators. The world's leading mathematician and physicist who recently passed away actively supported the United World Federalists, the organization so popular with college groups since World War II. Even the masses are internationally minded. It is a political asset for a politician to espouse internationalism today.

These toe nations which prophecy says will not cleave together until the time of the end (Daniel 2:43) are rapidly coming together now. When this coming together has fully jelled, the Scriptures teach that they will pledge their allegiance to one ruler who will be the ruler in power when Christ returns (Revelation 17:12, 13; Daniel 7:25, 26; Revelation 19:20). They assert that they need this cleaving together for collective security. Bible believers who watched for the fulfillment of prophecy after World War II did not have long to wait for the toe nations to start coming together. First it was the Atlantic Pact, then the North Atlantic Treaty Organization (NATO), then the Baghdad Pact. Recently there occurred an incident considered insignificant to the casual reader, but which prophecy students view with intense interest. The prime ministers of six of these nations in the territory to be federated at the time of the end, met in Paris and laid the groundwork for a community of nations comparable to the United States or Russia in power. They agreed to the establishment of a common market free from tariffs and trade barriers, to have a common atomic energy commission and to pool their atomic resources. This newest federation has not been named as yet. The prime ministers called it the "Paris concord."

There recently appeared in the daily press some comments by newsmen about this federation. This appeared in a column by Holmes Alexander in the *Greenville News:* "No signs are hung in the heavens when mankind passes from one historical phase to another. But it would be dangerous for American statesmen not to know the meaning of West Europe's proposed free-trade area of 280 million customers . . . Where do American interests lie? We will hardly be willing to fight another war to prevent Europe from uniting." From an editorial in the *Greenville News:* "Britain is watching with some concern the possibility that there may develop on the continent, given time and the right world conditions, a new power which she would either have to join or, in whose shadow, be content to dwell."

Our Secretary of State recently made the statement, "A United States of Europe is nearer than ever before." To students of prophecy this was nothing new. One of the two main contributions of World War II to the course of world history was to break down the nationalistic barriers and animosities and pave the way for the cleaving together of these toes of Daniel's image. World War II toppled England from her dominant position in Europe so that this federation can arise. This cleaving together is happening simultaneously with other world events which the prophetical Scriptures teach will happen at the time of the end of this age. There is an Israel today to make a covenant with this federation (Daniel 9:27). This was not so even twelve years ago. Israel is surrounded by bitter enemies and needs this covenant for protection. There is a strong growling Magog today manifesting her hatred toward Israel and ready to march against her and fulfill Ezekiel 38, 39. The chronology of prophecy and current world events are synchronizing like the teeth on geared wheels. How could anyone but the omnipotent God know in advance that these events would happen at all, much less simultaneously? The same God that foretold they would happen said they would happen at the time of the end. How can it be otherwise than the time of the end now?

According to prophetic chronology the stone cut out of the mountain will crush this image in the days of its toes. This stone kingdom represents the kingdom of heaven set up by Christ at His second coming. According to the Scriptures this stone will strike the toe kingdoms and break them to pieces when they are federated for a short time after long separation. Could it happen in the "days of these kings"? Is this it? Truly it is time for the child of God to give diligence to his consecration, to take care to be not conformed to this world, and to set his affections on things above. In view of prophetic truth, surely the kingdom of heaven is at hand.

CHAPTER III

THE END OF RUSSIA

> *And it shall come to pass in that day, that I will give unto Gog a place there of graves in Israel, the valley of the passengers on the east of the sea: and it shall stop the noses of the passengers: and there shall they bury Gog and all his multitude: and they shall call it the Valley of Hamon-gog.*—Ezekiel 39:11.

THE Battle of Armageddon is an appellation given to a great battle that will be fought at the end of this age, according to the Scriptures. The name of this battle is so well known that even those who are not familiar with the Bible refer to it often. It is a well-known fact that this battle will be fought when Christ meets the Antichrist and his armies at the end of this age and destroys them.

There is another great battle to be fought at the end of this age, that stands out just as prominently in the Holy Scriptures as the Battle of Armageddon, although it is almost unknown by the laity and hardly ever mentioned by ministers. The place where this battle will be fought, or at least the place where five-sixths of the hordes which invade Israel will be buried, will be called Hamon-gog. Moffatt's translation is as follows: "I will give Gog then a famous place for his grave within Israel, the Valley of Abarim, east of the Dead Sea; there shall they bury Gog and all his mob, and call it the Valley of Gog-mob."

In Ezekiel 38, 39 we find a truth that has often confused and baffled Bible students. We find that another federation of nations under a beastly leader, Gog, ruler of Magog, will also attack Israel at the end of the age. Because of the similarity of these battles and their close proximity, and in both, Israel's enemies are defeated by the providence of God, most Bible students erroneously conclude they are one and the same. There is nothing clearer in prophecy than the fact that these two federations of nations led by two different rulers comprise two distinct and different groups of nations. We know by the Scriptures that the beginning of the Antichrist federation will be the alliance of nations within the territory of the Roman Empire (Daniel 7:24-27; Revelation 17:12). They are the toes of Daniel's image, that God regards as the last stage of the Roman Empire. The leading nations of Gog's empire were never a part of the Roman Empire. This one fact alone is enough to prove that these two groups of nations which come against Israel in the end time are separate and distinct.

In Ezekiel 37 God foretells the regathering of Israel. The dry bones coming to life and being given sinews and clothed with flesh do not represent a revival of dry church members as is so often proclaimed in sermon and song. It is expressly declared that it represents the bringing of Israel up out of their graves and placing them back in their own land. After chapter 37 gives the assurance that there will be an Israel again in the end of the age, then chapters 38 and 39 give the assurance of the sequence of events that will follow. Gog, the ruler of Magog, as commander of the northern confederacy will come like a storm against Israel, like a cloud to cover the land (Ezekiel 38:8, 9). When Gog marches into Israel, God has promised He will put hooks in Gog's jaws (Ezekiel 38:4).

God begins the prophecy by stating, "I am against thee, O Gog, the chief prince of Mesheck and Tubal" (Ezekiel 38:3). The Septuagint, Moffatt's translation, and the American Standard Version render it: "Chief Prince of Rosh, Meshek, and Tubal." Dr. C. I. Scofield in his footnotes on Ezekiel 38 states: "That the primary reference is to the northern (European) powers, headed up by Russia, all agree. Gog is the prince, Magog his land. The reference to Meshek and Tubal (Moscow and Tobolsk) is a clear mark of identification." Dr. Scofield gives here the sum of the opinions of competent scholars arrived at after thorough research.

The new Schaff-Herzog *Encyclopedia of Religious Knowledge* (Volume 5, page 14) has this to say about the identity of Gog: "A people usually identified with the Scythians . . . a stricter geographical location would place Magog's dwelling between Armenia and Media, perhaps on the shores of the Araxes. But the people seem to have extended farther north across the Caucasus, filling the extreme northern horizon of the Hebrews."

Fausset's *Bible Encyclopedia* (page 445) has this to say of the people of Magog: "Mixed with the Medes they became the Sarmatians, whence sprang the Russians."

We know from the Bible that Magog was the second son of Japheth, who was the son of Noah (Genesis 10:1, 2). Dr. Louis S. Bauman, in his splendid book *Russian Events in the Light of Bible Prophecy*, has this to say: "Josephus, the great Jewish historian (Book I, Chapter VII), contemporaneous with Christ, said: 'Magog founded them that from his were named Magogites, but who by the Greeks were called Scythians.' The early Church fathers, Theodoret and Jerome, agree with Josephus. The Scythians themselves have a tradition that their ancestors originally came forth from Araxes, in Armenia. This concurs with the divine record which places the immediate descendants of Noah in Armenia. Historically speaking, the Scythians (Magogites) must have immigrated northward in very early times." Dr. Bauman further states: "Another early scholar, the eminent German Protestant Hebraist, Gesenius, whose Hebrew Lexicon has never been superseded, says that 'Gog is undoubtedly the Russians.' He declared that 'Rosh' was a designation for the tribes then north of the Taurus mountains, dwelling in the neighborhood of the Volga, and he held that in this name and tribe we have the first trace in history of the 'Russ,' or Russian nation. Gesenius also identified 'Meshech' as Moscow, the capital of modern Russia in Europe. 'Tubal' he identified as Tobolsk, the earliest province of Asiatic Russia to be colonized, and also the name of the city wherein Peter the Great built the old fortress after the pattern of the Kremlin at Moscow. Moscow bespeaks Russia in Europe and Tobolsk bespeaks Russia in Asia. Without doubt, Russia is the only nation in the world today that can even approach the role that 'Gog' is to play upon the state of the nations as 'the times of the gentiles' draws to a close."

We find in Ezekiel 38:5, 6 that Persia, Ethiopia, Libya, Gomer and Togarmah will march under Magog's leadership. It is not the writer's intention to identity all the nations led by Gog, the ruler of Magog, when he marches to his doom in Israel. The identities of the prominent ones are not controversial. Persia is easily recognized as modern Iran. Almost all encyclopedias and Bible dictionaries identify Gomer as modern Germany. Gomer was Japheth's eldest son and the father of those people known at the dawn of history as Cimmerians or the Gimirrai. Historians identify these Gimirrai, or Gimerii, of the cuneiform inscriptions as the first settlers of Crimea, and from there these Gimirrai migrated up the Danube and founded Germania, or modern Germany.

The difficulty arises with many Bible readers when they try to place Ethiopia and Libya in a northern confederacy. This seemingly insurmountable difficulty vanishes when we realize that through the centuries countries have changed names many times. Modern Iran and Iraq have been at various stages of their existence Babylon, Persia, and Assyria. The original Hebrew noun translated Ethiopia in the Authorized Version is *Kuwsh,* which Strong's Concordance identifies as Cush. The American Standard Revised Version and also Moffatt's translation renders *Kuwsh* as Cush.

The *Encyclopedia Americana* (1954 edition, volume 8, page 333) states that Cush could be in Africa or Arabia or represents "Kashshu, an old name for Babylonia."

The *Encyclopedia Britannica* (1954 edition, volume 6, page 901) says of Cush: "The exact territory thus designated is uncertain, some maintain it lies in Africa . . . others that it is in Arabie, while a third view again associates the name with the 'Kassites,' who for some centuries dominated Babylonia."

Likewise the difficulty arising from reading in the Authorized Version that Libya will march with Russia in a northern confederacy vanishes when we realize that in the original Hebrew text Libya in Africa was not referred to at all. The noun in the Hebrew text is *Puwt.* Strong's *Exhaustive Concordance of the Bible* has this to say of Puwt in Ezekiel 38:5, translated Libya in the King James Version: "Puwt;

Put, a son of Ham, also the name of his descendants or their region, and of a Persian tribe—Phut, Put." So we see that Strong's Concordance does not even consider Libya as a possible translation of Ezekiel 38:5, but identifies it as a region and name of a Persian tribe. Moffatt's translation agrees and reads Put instead of Libya. This harmonizes with prophecy and also current events which is the fulfillment of prophecy. Cush and Put, countries adjacent to Persia, will like Persia, be allied with Russia when they march to their doom in Israel's land. Most of these countries surrounding Israel are Moslems. We have seen the bitter hatred of these countries toward Israel manifested within the last few years and months and in one accord they have declared their unity in their efforts to throw Israel out of the land of their fathers. These Moslem nations are looking, with ever-increasing hope, toward Russia for help in their war against Israel, and Russia has taken her proper place in prophecy by arming Israel's enemies and taking her stand against Israel.

Someone may ask why the Bible is so confusing in naming the nations in the northern confederacy that is soon to come against Israel. The Bible was written for all generations, not just for our own. If the Bible had called the descendants of Magog Russia, it would have been more confusing to generations who lived before there was a Russia than Magog is to us today.

Let us look farther into the Scripture concerning the battle of Hamon-gog. It is acknowledged by most competent exegetes of whatever faith that the age will end by the return of the Lord with the raptured saints to destroy the Antichrist, who will be laying siege to exterminate Israel. There are so many Scriptures that clearly tell this that it is common knowledge amongst the laity of our generation (Daniel 7:24-27; Daniel 8:25; Revelation 19:17-21; 2 Thessalonians 2:8-11; Zechariah 14:2-12).

The Scriptures also state explicitly that this Antichrist or Beast will rule over the ten-toe federation, which is the last stage of the Roman Empire. Here is where the confusion comes in that has baffled students of the Word so consistently for many years. In Ezekiel 38, 39 we are told of an entirely different confederation occupying different parts of the earth coming down to besiege Israel in the end of the age just like the Roman or Antichrist federation (or the United States of Europe federation). This abortive attempt of this federation to exterminate Israel is thwarted by the interposition of God just as the intent of the Antichrist is thwarted.

Here we have the revelation that two federations near the same time (end of age) move against the same nation (Israel) and are defeated the same way (by interposition of God). Most exegetes have presumed that the same battle, the Battle of Armageddon, ends both of these federations and that the rulers of these federations are one and the same person. Yet it remains a clear fact in Scripture that these are two different and distinct federations, occupying different parts of the globe, and encompassing two different, distinct groups of nations that will try to exterminate Israel at the end of the age.

Some have tried to ignore the difficulty by presuming that Gog and the Antichrist are one and the same person and Gog's federation is the same as the Antichrist's federation. Others have tried to solve the problem by the conjecture that one ruler and his federation will conquer the other ruler and his federation and then march as one against Israel. Could not the confusion be cleared by disregarding the age-old tradition that there is but one great battle at the end of the age, the Battle of Armageddon? Where is there any Scripture that teaches that the Battle of Armageddon and the Battle of Hamon-gog are one and the same? In fact, when we look closer at the Scriptures we see that Magog (Russia) and the Antichrist kingdom do not end the same way. At the Battle of Hamon-gog it is expressly stated that Gog of Magog (Russia) will be a "guard unto them" or a commander unto them (Ezekiel 38:7). In the Battle of Armageddon it is stated that the Beast or Antichrist will be the commander (Revelation 19:19). In the Battle of Hamon-gog God calls for a sword to destroy Magog (Ezekiel 38:21). In the Battle of Armageddon the Lord shall go forth and fight against those nations as when He fought in the day of battle (Zechariah 14:3; 2 Thessalonians 2:8; Isaiah 63:3-6). In the Battle of Armageddon the Lord will not call for a sword, but will consume with the spirit of His mouth, and shall destroy with the brightness of His coming (2 Thessalonians 2:8).

In Ezekiel 38 God calls for His sword to destroy Magog's hordes. God in times past has used many heathen nations as His sword to accomplish His purpose. Babylon, Assyria, Persia, Rome and others were used by God to chastise Israel for their disobedience. Why could He not use the Antichrist federation (United Nations of Europe) to put a hook in Gog's jaws? In fact, the Scriptures teach plainly that during the last seven years of Israel's history before she accepts the true Messiah and the millennium starts, she will possess a covenant, or a treaty of protection, with the Antichrist, the ruler of the United Nations of Europe (Daniel 9:27). When the Magog (Russian) hordes march against her, no doubt she will invoke the covenant. Jesus, referring to this, said: "I am come in my Father's name, and ye receive me not: if another shall come in his own name, him ye shall receive" (John 5:43). One of the many facts that point to the nearness of the end of the age is the fact that Israel urgently needs that covenant today; she has her back to the wall, fighting for her existence against great numerical odds.

Another glaring sign that our redemption is near is the fact that these two federations are in existence and strong and already gearing for battle. The only difference in the conditions of these federations today and their condition at the end is that one of them, the European federation, needs a little more consolidating and the emergence of a strong ruler to which the individual rulers of the federation will pledge their allegiance (Daniel 7:24-27; Revelation 17:12, 13). Also, the ecclesiastical empire, represented by the Scarlet Woman in Revelation 17, and the political federation, represented by the ten-horned beast that carries her, will probably be a little closer in wedlock at the time of the end. The important thing to the child of God is that these conditions of the time of the end did not exist twenty years ago, but do exist and are congealing fast today. Yes, it vitally concerns us; it lets us know that our redemption draweth nigh!

When the Antichrist and his federation, with their atomic and hydrogen bombs and other mighty weapons, annihilate five-sixths of Magog's hordes, it is then he becomes exalted to the point of declaring himself to be God (2 Thessalonians 3:4) and will place the abomination of desolation, referred to by Daniel (Daniel 12:11) and Jesus (Matthew 24:15), and will break the covenant with Israel (Daniel 9:27). It is at this time Satan, by incarnating himself in this man, will make his supreme bid for open worship by the human race.

The abomination of desolation is first mentioned in Daniel. Jesus places the stamp of authenticity on Daniel by referring to this prophecy during His discourse on the end of the age and emphasizes that this event ushers in the very end. Paul, in 2 Thessalonians, throws more light on this abomination:

"Let no man deceive you by any means: for that day shall not come, except there come a falling away first, and that man of sin be revealed, the son of perdition; who opposeth and exalteth himself above all that is called God, or that is worshipped; so that he as God sitteth in the temple of God, shewing himself that he is God" (2 Thessalonians 2:3, 4). Then John unveils the mystery entirely in Revelation 13. There it is stated that the false prophet, the ecclesiastical ruler, makes an image to the beast, the political ruler, and demands all to worship the image and receive a mark. The Scriptures in both Matthew 24:15 and 2 Thessalonians 2:4 make it clear that the image will be in the rebuilt temple; therefore, the "abomination of desolation standing in the Holy Place." Satan at this time will produce real signs for a sign-hungry world. This image will speak and fire will fall from heaven. Someone may point to the fact that the temple does not exist today. In this age of modern technology and engineering, with a mighty empire subject to the Antichrist, it can be built in a phenomenally short time.

When could there be a more favorable time for the Antichrist to demand this sacrilege from Israel than when he delivers Israel from the siege of Russia? It is stated in Daniel 11:45 that it is after a great victory in battle at the very end of this age that he plants his palace between the seas in the glorious holy mountain.

For years there was a hoax perpetrated by international anti-Semitic forces that tried to identify Communism as a Jewish conspiracy. I well remember, as a young preacher before World War II, when a friend spoke to me in lowered tones about a booklet titled *The Protocols of the Wise Men of Zion.* This friend secured the book for me and slipped it to me in bootleg fashion as clandestine material. This was at the time Hitler was fanning the flames of hatred toward all Jews. This obnoxious fabrication declared that Communism was a Jewish conspiracy and that Zionism was seeking to promote a war among gentile nations, and bleed them white so Jews could rule the world and have gentiles as slaves. After the war it was proved that Hitler caused the book to be published.

It is true that Karl Marx, a Jew, wrote *Das Kapital,* the Communist Bible. He and Fredrick Engels composed the Communist Manifesto of 1848. There have been a few Jews in the ruling clique of Communism just as men of this fabulous race have found a niche in all other professions. Anti-Semites have made much of these coincidents. Neither God nor the race has ever claimed that there would never be Jewish renegades.

The bitter hatred and dissensions today that have the nations preparing to annihilate each other are not inspired by desire for each other's territory as in ages gone by. The hatred and fear that have torn the world asunder are caused by the death struggle between ideologies. The very things that are dear to

Israel are the things that Communism has vowed to fight to the death. Although Israel did not recognize the Messiah when He came the first time, the Jews have, nevertheless, been a thorn in Satan's side as a testimony to the one true and living God. Communism's hatred of Israel's God is well known. There is no other race so well fitted by their industry, endowments, and capacities to naturally resist Communism as the Jews. The Politburo fully recognizes this. They have declared Israel has no legal right to exist and that Zionism is synonymous with capitalism.

Within the last five years Russia's hatred of Israel has come out on the surface. Stalin, shortly before his death, accused the Jewish doctors of a plot to murder the Communist hierarchy and had them imprisoned. In the Suez episode the Russian Politburo threatened to unleash a rain of bombs on Israel if they did not stop fighting Egypt.

God said in the latter days that Magog would be "visited." In other words, Magog would be aroused or become powerful among the nations. For centuries Russia lay dormant like a sleeping giant. In 1905 little Japan thoroughly whipped her. Since 1917 Russia has been "visited." She has gained importance and power by leaps and bounds. What nation today does not fear the Russian might? Her people have been deprived of consumer goods for years so that a mighty army might be equipped with super cannons, super tanks, and super bombs.

The pattern of Communist aggression in the past

has been to advance where they could gain the most by expending the least. The industry of returned Israel is sure to produce wealth that will be coveted by Magog. God said she would say, "I will go to them that are at rest . . . To take a spoil and to take a prey; to turn thine hand upon the desolate places that are now inhabited, and upon the people that are gathered out of the nations, which have gotten cattle and goods that dwell in the midst of the land" (Ezekiel 38:11, 12).

The Russian giant is poised to strike, and according to the immutable Word the supreme effort will not be in Europe or the Far East, or over the North Pole. The Russian might will be humbled and slain in Israel's land, and will be buried in a valley in Israel which from henceforth will be known as Hamongog.

Great military minds may not agree to this. Many of us remember when Hitler marched against Russia how many experts predicted Russia would fall in a short time. One nationally known person said Russia would fall in three weeks. Yet, while Hitler's panzer divisions were sweeping through Russia, students of prophecy who believe that the end of the age is near predicted that when the smoke of battle rolled away Russia would be the victor. They based their prediction on the Scripture that states that Magog will be a guard (commander) of the northern confederacy and Gomer will be a follower. History has vindicated their faith in the prophetical Scriptures.

When Russia thinks this evil thought and marches into Israel, God said His fury shall come up into His face (Ezekiel 38:18) and He will call for a sword (the Antichrist confederation of nations) and will plead against Gog with pestilence, blood, hailstones, fire and brimstone, also every man's sword shall be against his brother. When five-sixths of this mighty mob falls on the open fields of Israel, Israel will be seven months burying Gog's mob (Ezekiel 39:5, 12).

In conclusion, may I ask why did not the rebirth of Israel and the "visiting" or becoming strong of Russia happen one hundred or five hundred years apart? The answer is that it was clearly stated both would happen in the latter years, or last years of the age. Thirty years ago Russia was too weak to march. Twelve years ago there was no Israel for her to march against. Today the stage is set for the final drama of Ezekiel 38, 39 to be enacted.

CHAPTER IV

THE MYSTERY OF BABYLON

> *And there came one of the seven angels which had the seven vials, and talked with me, saying unto me, Come hither; I will shew unto thee the judgment of the great whore that sitteth upon many waters.*
>
> *And upon her forehead was a name written, MYSTERY, BABYLON THE GREAT, THE MOTHER OF HARLOTS AND ABOMINATIONS OF THE EARTH.*—Revelation 17:1, 5.

HERE in Revelation 17 we have what many Bible students call the most mysterious chapter in the Bible. It is hard for a child of God to conceive that God gave the book of Revelation to mystify or confuse His children. Some claim that this book is not to be read or understood. This is also impossible for a Spirit-filled child of God to believe—that God placed it in the Bible just to fill in, especially in light of the assertion that "Blessed is he that readeth and they that hear the words of this prophecy," Revelation 1:3.

The book is highly symbolical, but these symbols are not haphazardly inserted; they are used consistently with their usage in other books of the Bible. For instance, the symbol of a horn represents a ruler of a realm. The ten horns in Revelation 17 represent ten kings or kingdoms just as the ten horns in Daniel 7:7 represent the ten rulers who are subordinate to the Antichrist. The two horns on the ram of Daniel 8:3 represent the dual kingdom, Medo-Persia, and the horn in the forehead of the he goat of Daniel 8:5 represents Alexander the Great, the founder of the Grecian Empire.

The interpretation of Revelation should never be farfetched and fantastic or in contradiction to other Scriptures. The last book of the Bible is not the book of John the Revelator, neither is it the book of Revelations. It is the book of Revelation. It reveals conditions that will exist just before, at the time, and immediately after the return of Jesus Christ. It reveals Christ's second coming.

The seven-headed, ten-horned beast and the Scarlet Woman of Revelation 17 represent something of world importance that will exist at the end of the age. Without doubt, that means today. We know God wanted us to understand the mystery, because the angel told John, "I will tell thee the mystery of the woman, and of the beast that carrieth her, which hath the seven heads and ten horns." The angel proceeded to tell what the beast, the heads, the horns, and the waters represented. The Beast is a term in the Scriptures synonymous with the Antichrist and is used for both the person and his empire. Verse 3 refers to the empire, while verse 8 refers to the person. It is thrilling to know the mysteries God unfolds in His Word, yet I will not elaborate on verse 8 as it is controversial and is not necessarily conducive to consecration.

There may be cause for controversy concerning the meaning of the heads of the beast, but the Scriptures leave no room for speculation concerning the meaning of the ten horns on the beast and the waters on which the woman sitteth. It is plainly stated, "The waters which thou sawest, where the whore sitteth, are peoples, and multitudes, and nations, and tongues," Revelation 17:15. In view of this revelation, any fair unbiased interpretation will have to admit, whatever the woman is, she is a human institution that exists in many nations. Then verse 12 tells us that the ten horns represent ten kings (or rulers) which receive power one hour (short time) with the Beast. The Scripture here interprets itself. If the ten horns are ten rulers who unite and give their power for a short time to the Beast, or Antichrist, then the ten-horned beast represents the Antichrist government. These horns are identical with the ten toes of Daniel 2:40-45 where it is revealed that the Antichrist's government which Christ will break to pieces at His second coming will be composed of a union of nations which are part of the fragments of the Roman Empire. The thing that thrills us today is to know that this union is now forming. The Beast carrying the woman and the woman riding the Beast show the close affinity of the United States of Europe and this woman at the end of the age. This woman will be powerful enough to be upheld by the Beast because of the service she can render in bringing him and his government into power. She will be indispensable to him.

In the Scriptures a woman represents a religious economy or a religious system. An adulterous woman is the symbol God uses to represent backslidden Israel in Ezekiel 16 and Hosea 2. Most Bible scholars believe the woman in Revelation 12 is Israel, while some believe she is the true Church. God revealed to Paul and John that Christ would have a bride who is the true Church (Ephesians 3:6-12; 5:30, 31; Revelation 19:7). The Scripture reveals here in Revelation 17 that Satan will have a bride. This woman will have to have an extensive, powerful government if she is able to help unite the fragments of Rome and propel herself into power as co-ruler with the Beast. May I ask what human institution is extensive enough and powerful enough in the geographical territory of the Roman Empire to help consolidate the United States of Europe? It certainly is not Communism, for Communism and the Antichrist will be deadly enemies and clash in Palestine when Russia marches against Israel. Search as we may, there is only one institution strong enough to fulfill this Scripture. This Scarlet Woman can be none other than apostate Christendom and false religions headed up by Roman Catholicism. Every one of the nations within the territory of the Roman Empire which recently formed a union and agreed to eliminate tariffs and trade barriers, and

THE MYSTERY OF BABYLON

work together for the common interest, is dominated by Roman Catholicism. At this time this woman will realize the dream she has schemed to make come true for centuries, the dream that was interrupted by the Reformation; she will become the state religion of a mighty empire.

God gives a complete history of the gentile world governments and also a history of the future of Israel in the prophetical Scriptures. Prophecy would not be complete without the history of the church in advance. God gave this foreview in Revelation 2 and 3. In these chapters God gives a message to seven churches which had conditions in them representative of seven periods of the church age. In the Ephesus age, the first church age, God said they had the deeds of Nicolaitans. Scofield, in his footnotes, says Nicolaitane comes from *Nikao*, "to conquer" and *Laos*, "the people." This foretells the priestly assumption of power. In the Pergamos, or third church age, the deeds had become a doctrine (Revelation 2:15). In the Thyatiraian, or fourth age, this priestly assumption of power was fully organized into an apostate church which God called "that woman Jezebel." This Thyatiraian age, when this woman ruled supremely, lasted from the fourth century until 1517, when Martin Luther and his contemporaries began the Sardis age, or Reformation age. God said He gave her space to repent and she repented not, therefore He will cast her into great tribulation (the great tribulation).

Revelation 13 tells us that the second beast, or false

prophet, will make an image to the first beast, or Antichrist, and cause all to worship the image and take the mark or be killed. This false prophet will be the high pontiff of the state church. The two horns, true to scriptural symbolism, represent his political and ecclesiastical power.

This woman began as the Babylonian cult in the Babylonian Empire. Here in the cradle of the human race Satan injected the embryo of all false religions. The members joined a mystical brotherhood and gave allegiance to a high pontiff. When this satanic religion was forced from Babylon by the conquering Persians, the pontiff fled to Pergamos in Asia Minor (Revelation 2:13). From there the Etruscans migrated with this religion to Italy where Julius Caesar became the first Roman high pontiff of the cult. When the Emperor Gratian refused the office, it was given to Damascus, the bishop of Rome. The Roman church apostatized and Babylonian Cultism was mixed with a few Christian doctrines and became Mystery Babylon, the mother of harlots and abominations of the earth. Even the colored vesture of the priests of this church corresponds to the scarlet and purple robes of this woman. Everything pertaining to this woman is permeated with mystery. There is the mystery of the holy water, the mystery of purgatory, the mystery of transubstantiation.

There is a subtle scheme to persuade the American people that we need to lock arms with Catholicism because she is a bulwark against Communism. This

THE MYSTERY OF BABYLON

scheme has been very successful. How can these schemers explain the fact that *every country in Europe that has gone Communist was first dominated by the Catholic Church?*

The largest Communist party outside of Russia is in Italy, the very fountainhead of Catholicism. Only by a dole of millions of American dollars has Italy been prevented from going completely Communist. Then we are told we have to go against our American tradition, our consciences, and the Bible because the Catholic Church is a bulwark against Communism. Those who advocate embracing Catholicism to escape Communism remind us of the Scripture in which "a man did flee from a lion, and a bear met him; or went into the house and leaned his hand on the wall, and a serpent bit him," Amos 5:19. An editorial from the *Christian Advocate,* official publication of North Carolina Methodist Church, stated recently: "If, in our zeal to protect ourselves from the menace of Communism we come under the domination of a particular religious denomination, we shall, indeed, have traded our birthright for a tyranny fully as unacceptable to our principles as Communism itself."

Satan has our generation in a giant pincers movement between Communism and Catholicism. He is winning in the East with Communism and in the West with Catholicism. This, too, is according to the Scripture. Communism rules in the nations which will be led by Magog (Ezekiel 38, 39). Catholicism rules in the ten nations which will confederate under Antichrist. The same God who said He was against Gog of Magog (Russia) and that He would put hooks in his jaws also said He was against that woman Jezebel of the dark ages, who is the Scarlet Woman of the end time, and would cast her into great tribulation.

As it nears the end of the age this woman will increase in power until she will "ride" the Beast or be co-ruler with the Beast. That is just what is happening today and this woman is gaining in power by leaps and bounds. Every country in Europe purchased from Communism by American dollars has been turned over to the Catholic Church, which she governs through her political front organizations. Where the Catholic Church dominates a country, religious freedom suffers as much or more than under Communism. The true gospel is hated and suppressed as much or more under Catholicism than under Communism.

The Catholic Church gives lip service to tolerance in America because it is in the minority. In European and Latin-American countries where the church is in the saddle, tolerance is unknown. Many of you are aware of the inhuman atrocities perpetrated against Protestants in South American countries by Catholicism.

In many European countries civil rulers cannot rule without Catholic approval. This is why the Beast's government will "carry" the woman. In some of these countries the papacy rules through absolute dictatorship. Catholicism favors dictators if the dictators favor Catholicism. It chooses and dethrones rulers at will. Argentina and Colombia are two recent examples. The sinister power of this Woman is reflected in the press and news media of the world. As long as these dictators are favored by the papal system they are praised by the press. When they are dethroned, then the press defames them. A captive press is as dangerous to real liberty as a secret police force or the bayonets of a dictator.

I have before me an article from the associated press dated New York, May 5, 1957, which asserts that "a Roman Catholic group is actively engaged in censorship of what the American people may read." This article says more than 150 prominent persons in the fields of publishing literature, and the arts signed the statement which says that a reading community of mothers of the Roman Catholic faith in the Chicago area evaluates literature as to its suitability for youth. The article continues by saying this group has "prepared black lists, threatened and imposed general boycotts and awarded unofficial certificates of compliance."

Catholicism, under the subterfuge of separation of church and state, has had power to separate the Bible from American public schools. A few years ago the Supreme Court of New Jersey ruled that the Gideons could not give away Bibles in the public schools of that state. This Woman will go to any extreme to shield her subjects from contact with the Bible. The hierarchy knows that the truth can set them free.

This Woman is flexing her muscles as the end of

the age nears. It is nothing but right in a democracy that Catholics and all other minorities should have a fair representation in the branches of our government. It is not only morally wrong, but dangerously wrong that they have such disproportionate power in America.

I have before me an article from the United Press dated Chicago, May 31, 1957, in which Glen L. Archer, speaking at the recent Southern Baptist National Convention, compared "Roman Clericalism" to the Red threat. Mr. Archer blasted the directive of Connecticut Archbishop O'Brien of Hartford which he said "asks Catholics of that state to exert political pressure on state legislators and take reprisal against any who did not vote for a bill granting state funds to Catholic schools." According to the Scripture, when this Woman is firmly entrenched in power, these reprisals will consist of the death sentence, and her "certificate of compliance" will be a visible mark (Revelation 13:16).

This woman sits upon many waters, which are "peoples, multitudes, nations and tongues." She never ceases her tireless activities in many countries to regain her power lost by the Reformation. She is boring from within to gain control of American institutions. She boasts of taking a leaf from the Communist book and of having her people at the right place at the time voting is done or policy changes occur in labor unions. In America she masquerades as a champion of the laboring people. In large labor convocations the invocation is nearly always given by a Catholic priest. In countries where she has absolute power, when her civil rulers favor the working people, she will depose them as she did Peron of Argentina when he turned pro-labor.

We are in an age of high literacy when periodicals and the press wield a mighty influence in molding the opinion of people in political and other affairs. The Catholic Church is exerting a mighty influence in this field. Many periodicals have been used to advance the cause of this Scarlet Woman.

In 1950 the high pontiff gave a decree for judges who are members of this church to let church law supersede national law in whatever country they may sit as judges. I do not wish to give a blanket indictment here. I believe many are patriotic and true to their oath of office. All I say is that the decree was given. The terrible potential is very clear.

Most Catholic laymen in America are sincere in their religion, having been shielded from the truth from infancy. They are upright American citizens. It is the hierarchy that knows what the goal is and is executing the plans. While Protestants consider the spiritual realm their legitimate field of operation, Romanism has many alphabetical agencies to advance her interests in politics, propaganda, and intrigue.

A minister friend of the writer was a chaplain in the United States Army in World War II. He relates that he became an intimate friend of Catholics in the Army who arrogantly stated that the South is their greatest missionary opportunity. They also stated that one of their methods is to bring many immigrant families to the United States, settle them in one community, then instruct them to marry Protestants but marry in the Catholic Church. It was stated that by this method they could completely break down the Protestant tradition. We do know that these immigrant settlements are being made.

In the countries this Woman dominates she does not have to have so many fronts; she operates openly in the political arena under innocent-sounding n a m e s. Many people are deluded by this. After all, this has to be. This woman will "ride" the ten-horned European Beast.

No doubt the papacy will be the leader of apostate religions, but not the whole. She is the mother of harlots. Many apostate religions will come under her wings in the end time. There has been an amalgamation mania abroad in the world in recent years. The fashion in church circles today is to amalgamate. Unity is held out as a virtue within itself. Apostate Christendom will have to be confederated to the point where one supreme pontiff (the false prophet) can pull the reins. Many close their eyes to the fact that divergence of belief and freedom of interpretation have kept the truth from being stifled in the strait jacket of a state church. No doubt when this unity has congealed in the end time it will mutate into conformity. The high pontiff has already issued the invitation for the "erring" ones to return. Most Americans would be shocked to know how many leaders in nominal Christendom hold this desired unity to be of greater importance than the truths which caused separation.

No lesser authority than the great Arnold Toynbee concludes that religion in itself is good for men—not any particular brand—just religion. His prognosis, so highly esteemed by many, is that Buddhism, Mohammedanism, Taoism, Catholicism, and all other "isms" are on a plane with Christianity and in the end the race will progress in wisdom until all religions will unite in a conglomerated system. Although he does not base them on the Scripture, his predictions here are uncanny. There will be a conglomerated state church for the Confederated States of Europe. The two-horned ecclesiastical ruler, no doubt, will be the Scarlet Woman's high pontiff and the object of worship will be the Beast or Antichrist.

This union of church and state will continue until the Beast becomes the sole object of worship; then his government shall "hate the whore, and shall make her desolate and naked, and shall eat her flesh, and burn her with fire" (Revelation 17:16). This will be the fulfillment of God's promise to cast her into the great tribulation. The full development of the ten-horned beast and the woman riding him is seen near by the discerning Bible student. The rapture of the true church is also seen near at hand.

It is time for those who have fellowship with Jesus Christ to nestle a little closer to Him. All these things tell us plainly that the most momentous event in two thousand years is near—the second coming of Jesus Christ, the Son of God, the Prince of Peace, the Hope of the world.

CHAPTER V

THE MIRACLE OF THE JEW

> *What advantage then hath the Jew? or what profit is there of circumcision?*
> *Much every way: chiefly, because that unto them were committed the oracles of God.*
> —Romans 3:1, 2.
>
> *I say then, Hath God cast away his people? God forbid. For I also am an Israelite, of the seed of Abraham, of the tribe of Benjamin.*
> *God hath not cast away his people which he foreknew.*
>
> *For if thou wert cut out of the olive tree which is wild by nature, and wert graffed contrary to nature into a good olive tree: how much more shall these, which be the natural branches, be graffed into their own olive tree?*—Romans 11:1, 2, 24.

SECULAR history records the achievements and progress of particular races and nations telling how they arose, what territories they occupied, in what manner they were governed, what battles they fought, and how they fell. Profane history follows the trail of great conquerors and mighty empires. Not so with sacred history; God sees the human race in three categories: Jew (Israel), gentile (non-Hebrews), and the Church of God (God's called-out ones from both Jews and gentiles). Secular history is only written about past events. God, in sacred history, writes the history of these three categories of the race in advance. Before this history transpires it is called prophecy; after it transpires it becomes secular history. Consequently, because of our position in time a large part of the prophecies concerning these three categories of the human race has transpired and is now secular history. Yet there remains part of the history of these three categories of the race which is yet future and is therefore prophecy. If the student of Scripture understands the predestined history of these three categories of the race, it is a great asset in understanding world-shaking current events and helps him to even anticipate future world events.

In the succeeding chapters I wish to deal with the history both past and future of these three divisions of humanity: the Jew, the gentile, and the Church. The larger part of the prophetical history of these three categories of the race has transpired and has become authentic secular history. How then can any honest seeker of truth, however sceptical he may be, doubt that the remainder of this prophecy according to every jot and tittle will transpire?

When the human race, because of their depraved nature inherited from the first Adam, had become so vile that the whole earth was corrupted, God destroyed all but a seed of the race. Because of one righteous man eight persons were spared to propagate the race. As soon as the earth began to be replenished again the race reverted back into gross depravity. They did not wish to retain God in their knowledge. "They glorified him not as God, neither were thankful; but became vain in their imaginations, and their foolish heart was darkened" (Romans 1:21, 28). Because they preferred to worship dumb idols made like unto beasts rather than the merciful, omnipotent God, God gave them up to a reprobate mind. The race sank into the utterly depraved and subhuman conditions described in the first chapter of Romans.

From the midst of these depraved idolaters God chose Abram and commanded him to forsake his kindred and home to go to a new land and be the progenitor of a God-worshipping nation. God chose a special nation for a specific purpose, that purpose being the redemption of the race. God's purpose was to use this nation to bear testimony of the one true and living God to a depraved, idolatrous world. Their task was to reveal His nature to man and also to be the nation from which the Messiah, the Saviour of all men, would come.

Because we have inherited four thousand years of traditional monotheism and because of the effect the gospel has had on the world we cannot grasp the dismal abyss in which the human mind was bound at this time. Idolatrous, depraved polytheism was a universal state. We can better grasp the conditions if we can visualize the whole world today as being in the spiritual state of the most ignorant tribes in the hinterlands of Africa or South America. The gulfs between fallen man's depraved conception of deity and the glorious exalted nature of the omnipotent, omniscient, omnipresent, self-existent God was so wide that of necessity God's revelation of Himself was gradual and progressive. God's object in the call of the Hebrew nation was to reveal to them, and through them to the entire race, Himself as Creator, Sovereign, Father and Redeemer.

An early Hebrew concept of the Creator was expressed in the name *Ruach,* which denotes breath or spirit. The dumb idols were visible objects confined to one place at a time. Ruach, as Spirit, was invisible and omnipresent. Another step in progressive revelation is *Elohim.* This denotes High God, incomparable power, nothing He could not do. Another step in this revelation is *Qodesh.* This reveals the transcendence of the Eternal. He was separate, apart from, dwelling wholly beyond. The English equivalent is "holy." The idol gods were supposed to possess all the evil passions of fallen man. Even the gods of the highly civilized Greeks were jealous, wrathful, deceitful, adulterous, and murderous. The living God is holy. Another important step in this self-revelation of God is the name *Tsedeq.* This denotes ethical monotheism. Ethical originally meant moral. The one true living God is concerned with right and wrong. He has a norm or a standard which concerns morality. This points up the sin question. This was something absolutely unknown to the postdiluvian world at this time until this revelation to the Hebrew nation. The idol gods had no norm or standard.

It is true that the Spirit of Him who lighteneth every man that cometh into the world penetrated even the darkness of the heathen world to the extent that the Greek philosophers, such as Socrates and Plato, taught certain values of morality. Nevertheless, the idea of an individual's immoral acts displeasing a holy God and the truth of conversion and mystical union with a God that lives was unknown outside the Hebrew religious system.

The Eternal gave a moral code to Israel during the Exodus, the heart of which is the Ten Commandments. When this moral code was given, man discovered that deep in his nature was an inbred principle that rebelled against this moral standard of a holy God. This sin nature in man created a great gulf between man and a holy God. Here the Eternal reveals Himself as *Goel,* which is Redeemer: God of Salvation. *Redeem* is equivalent to buying back. It is the nature of God to buy back the sinner sold under sin. Now in the progressive self-revelation the Eternal appears to Israel as *Chesed*. This reveals God as a God of covenant love; determined to keep a covenant. A close English word is *grace*. Miles Coverdale translated it *loving kindness*. When the sin nature prevented man from obeying God's moral law, God provided the system of animal sacrifices and promised a new covenant. He promised to send His Son, the mighty God, the everlasting Father, the Prince of Peace to be wounded for man's transgression, to be bruised for man's iniquities, to be chastised for man's peace, and to be striped for man's healing (Isaiah 9:6; 55:5). The hundreds of thousands of animal sacrifices offered by the Hebrew nation were *proto-evangelium.* They pointed to the perfect Sacrifice offered once for all that would clear man's conscience and bring him into fellowship with the Eternal. The most exalted emotional experience known to man, the experience of conversion and mystical union with God, first appears in this chosen race, the Jews. Religious conversion first appears in recorded history in the Hebrew Bible.

It is hard to understand how Christians, or at least nominal Christians, can speak disparagingly about these chosen people and show animosity toward them. Although they were elected to serve as an instrument to bring the plan of salvation to the whole race, yet this election is unconditional. When God promised blessings on this people, He confirmed it with an oath (Hebrews 6:13, 14). They are the apple of His eye (Zechariah 2:8). He formed them for Himself (Isaiah 43:21). Although they have been chastised many times for their disobedience, they will never be cast off forever. Their choice is irrevocable. It is true they have been disobedient and even rejected the Messiah through unbelief, yet it was to this nation the Messiah was born. We should never forget that salvation is of the Jews (John 4:22). Paul says we, the grafted gentile branches, should never boast against the Jews, the natural branches. By the grace of God through His loving kindness they were broken off that we might receive salvation by faith, but the Scriptures are quick to state that they are not cast away forever. God is able to graft the natural branches back again (Romans 11:23). If the fall of them has been the riches of the gentiles, how much more their fulness (Romans 11:12)? In the family of God the Jews are compared to the root and fatness of the olive tree and gentile Christians as the branches. In other words, the whole Judeo-Christian culture that the world enjoys today had its beginning in the ancient past in this called-out chosen nation. Almost all codes of justice today, especially the Anglo-Saxon code, had their origin in the moral code that governed and shaped the Jewish nation.

All through the Hebrew Bible the Word of God is faithful in relating the shortcomings of this nation and does not fail to expose the sins of its greatest heroes such as David. Yet in the past dark night of universal idolatry, they held high the glorious light of ethical monotheism. Some seem to forget that in the dark past Israel was the only champion of Jehovah, while the world wallowed in orgies of sin and gross darkness. While the race was not perfect before the holy God and was chastised many times, yet there were heroes among them that in the dark hours of universal idolatry faced lions' dens and fiery furnaces to testify to the greatness of the one living God. To this nation was committed the oracles of God. It protected these oracles and preserved them as a precious legacy for humanity. They held high the torch of the living God in times of world-wide idolatry. Israel in its imperfect state was, in comparison to the depraved nations which surrounded it, a heavenly people. Through this nation the world was taught the fact of the existence of one true Creator God and was given a concept of His nature. The most perfect revelation of God that the human race has ever known was in Jesus Christ who came into the world as one of this race.

It is true that the Jews rejected Him; however, through this rejection the glorious grace of God came to the gentiles. Blindness in part came to them until the full gathering of the gentiles be come in (Romans 11:25). Because of this rejection they were dispersed over the entire earth, but they have been miraculously preserved as a distinct race. This is one of the greatest miracles in history. Here we see the race broken into fragments and scattered to the four winds of the earth, yet for nineteen hundred years they have remained as homogenous as any race in the world. God is not through with them; they have been cast off only for a period. One of the most emphasized truths in prophecy is the divine promise that Israel will be restored to their own land. It is made plain in Holy Writ that this restoration will be in the last of this age. In almost every prophecy concerning the regathering it is stated that it will take place in the last days (of this age). This restoration is in full swing today.

According to the Scriptures they are to be converted and yet see their greatest glory as a nation. They will be the head of the nations and not the tail in the near future (Deuteronomy 28:13). The promise of God that Israel would possess the land from the Nile to the Euphrates (Genesis 15:18) has not yet been fulfilled, but will be during her kingdom age. The world beholds an Israel again, but an unconverted Israel. The Scriptures teach that they will be converted during the tribulation week, the most terrible week in earth's history. This period is known as "the time of Jacob's trouble."

This is where Israel is today in the divinely inspired history of her existence. She is at the threshold of the great tribulation. Her troubles will grow worse until she will seek security by an alliance with the ruler of the confederated nations in the territory of old Rome. Unknown to her at first, this will be a covenant with the Antichrist. In the middle of the last week of the times of the gentiles this ruler will break his covenant with Israel and then Israel's agony will begin (Daniel 9:27). During this time of desperation and agony Israel will call on their God and a remnant will be saved and sealed (Revelation 7:4-8). At the close of earth's greatest convulsion, when many nations have surrounded Israel for the purpose of exterminating her (Zechariah 14:2) their Messiah, our Saviour, will return and deliver them with the brightness of His coming and glory of His power (2 Thessalonians 2:8; Zechariah 14:12). Then will come the kingdom for which they have longed for many centuries, the literal kingdom of heaven. The resurrected glorified saints of God will rule on earth with God's Son, Jesus Christ, but Israel will be God's earthly people and will reach and surpass her former glory during this one thousand years' reign.

Israel might, therefore, be labeled as God's irrefutable timepiece as regarding prophecy. It is reiterated time and again in prophetical Scriptures that Israel will be regathered in the last days. This means the last days of this age; the age of grace; the church age. Some who wish to deny the imminence of the Lord's second coming erroneously contend that this present rebirth of Israel is not the regathering of the last days. They contend that at the last days' regathering Israel will be converted. The teaching of this school is: Israel will be converted just before the regathering or at the exact time of regathering. They infer that Israel will return because her people will be converted. This is absolutely contradictory to the divine revelation. Just before their terrible suffering that hastens their conversion they will make a covenant with the Antichrist. In fact, the breaking of this covenant by the Antichrist signals the beginning of Jacob's trouble (Deuteronomy 30:7). There will have to be a self-governed Israel in order for them to make a covenant with the Beast. It is absurd to insinuate that the Beast could make a treaty with a people dispersed over the earth and assimilated among all nations without a government or a ruler. In fact, this is the hour Israel faces today. She is threatened from every side and is in dire need of a treaty of protection from some source. The very fact that Israel will make a treaty with the "man of sin" is proof enough that they will not return as a converted people trusting in Jesus Christ their King, but just the opposite.

When Jesus of Nazareth came at His first advent He fulfilled the prophecies of centuries concerning Himself. They saw Him do the works that no other man had ever done. They beheld Him open blind eyes, unstop deaf ears, cleanse the leper, and raise the dead. They testified that they never heard a man speak like this man. Even after He conquered death and came out of the tomb they could not believe this was the momentous hour, that this was He that should come. They continued to look for another. In like manner the same attitude is prevalent in the world today. When this great event has arrived—this promised return of Israel, this event that is the central theme of a great portion of the prophetical Scriptures, the event that God declares will be a sure sign of the end of the age—man, true to his nature, fails to see it and believe it.

There are some who profess to know and teach the Word who proclaim that this is not the return foretold in God's Word. They teach to look for another return. They minimize the importance of this momentous event and thereby minimize the urgency of being ready for the soon return of Christ. This school declares that this is an insignificant return, that there will be a more significant return.

When the facts are duly considered, how could it be possible for there to be a more significant return than the return that gave political rebirth to the nation? After nearly 2,000 years of being scattered among the nations, without a national home or a government, the seed of Abraham suddenly returned and there is a fully autonomous Israel in the midst of the nations again. If ten times as many should return, it would only increase the population of Israel; it would not alter the fact, or even add to the fact that the political rebirth of Israel happened on a day in 1948. The miracle of the return of Israel cannot be minimized in the light of the prophetical Scriptures. It was the most momentous event to transpire in 2,000 years. The significant fact is that the gentiles relinquished their power over the Holy Land after 2,000 years of rule and the miraculous Jews returned as a full-blooded and distinct race and re-established Israel after being "buried" 1,900 years among the nations. There can be a greater number return but there cannot be a more significant return.

It is taught nowhere in Scripture that there will be two regatherings at the end of this age; neither is it taught that one regathering will be insignificant and prepare the way for a more important regathering. In the numerous prophecies proclaiming the regathering of Israel at the end of this age it is never referred to as two regatherings or two phases of regathering. It is a well-known fact that the seed of Abraham are continuing to return, and the population is increasing at a phenomenal rate. Yet the all-important event was the political rebirth of the nation and the fact that there *is* an Israel.

The theory that there will be a future more important regathering of Israel before the second coming of Jesus Christ is bolstered by the unscriptural premise that Israel will have a spiritual rebirth before, or at the exact time of, the regathering. The Scriptures teach the exact opposite. As has been stated previously, when there is an Israel again in the last days of this age they will make a covenant with the Antichrist (Daniel 9:27). This shows that they are unconverted and have not accepted the true Christ. In fact, it is "the time of Jacob's trouble," the great tribulation, that will cause returned Israel to seek God and to accept their Messiah. In Jeremiah 30:3 the Spirit of prophecy declares that the day will come when God will bring again the captivity of His people and cause them to return to the land He gave to their fathers. The fifth verse declares that after this return there will be heard a voice of trembling, of fear, and not of peace. The sixth verse proclaims that every man will be in travail and all faces turned into paleness. The Scriptures declare these conditions to exist after they return, so we see the kingdom of peace does not begin immediately. Why this travailing, trembling and paleness? "Alas! for that day is great, so that none is like it: it is even the time of Jacob's trouble, but he shall be saved out of it" (Jeremiah 30:7). How shall Jacob be saved out of it? "For it shall come to pass in that day, saith the Lord of hosts, that I will break his yoke from off thy neck . . ." (Jeremiah 30:8). What is meant by *his* yoke? The pronoun *his* refers to the Antichrist, the last and most terrible ruler to dominate Israel. So we see that the Antichrist yoke will be upon Israel for a short time after they return. It is later that they are converted and accept Him whose yoke is easy and whose burden is light.

Many competent Bible students believe that it is the preaching of the two witnesses that helps to convert Israel. The two witnesses preach during the great tribulation, so if this be so, it is another proof that Israel is not converted until the tribulation week. This means that the Lord will return at the first phase of His second coming and rapture the Church before Israel is converted.

Israel has reached a crucial point in her long, glorious, tragic history. A certain amount of trembling and paleness already prevails. She is in dire need of a covenant with a strong federation to protect her from her enemies headed by Magog (Russia). Israel is facing her darkest hour, but immediately after that dark hour the glorious dawn will come. Christ will restore at that time the kingdom to Israel. Israel shall yet see her finest hour.

CHAPTER VI

TIMES OF THE GENTILES

> *And they shall fall by the edge of the sword, and shall be led away captive into all nations: and Jerusalem shall be trodden down of the Gentiles, until the times of the Gentiles be fulfilled.*—Luke 21:24.

THE Scriptures declare that known unto God are all of His works from the beginning of the world. The power of foreknowledge possessed by the omniscient God staggers the faith of some people. It is hard for puny man, with his finite mind, to grasp the infinite power of the eternal God. Some nominal Christians even claim to have an aversion to the prophetical Scriptures. They assert that we should be occupied with the principles of the doctrine of Christ such as repentance from dead works, faith towards God, the doctrine of baptisms, etc. These principles are certainly essential to salvation, but the Scriptures teach us that after we are partakers of these principles we can go on to deeper things (Hebrews 6:1). Paul makes it plain that Christians should develop beyond the "milk stage" of babes and grow in grace until they can enjoy strong meat (1 Corinthians 3:1, 2). It is one of the most thrilling experiences that we can have to know that God has taken us into His intimate councils and let us know the future. If one knows the history of the gentile nations in advance, he can understand the meaning of momentous current events and anticipate future events, while the learned in this world's wisdom who do not have faith in the Scriptures flounder in perplexity about the course future events will take.

In a broad sense all non-Hebrews are gentiles, but those gentiles who with Jews make up the Church are in the sight of God in an entirely different category of the race. The gentiles have occupied the center of the world stage for centuries. The time of the gentiles began in 606 B.C. when Judah was carried into Babylon by Nebuchadnezzar. During most of the centuries since that time, Palestine has been under the domination of the gentiles. The gentile nations have occupied the pages of secular history until the present time. During those years when the Israelites were in the land of promise, they were under the power of the gentiles, and at the time of the Saviour's birth Palestine was under the heavy hand of the taxing Romans.

While the Jewish nation was humbled by the power of Babylon and Daniel was still in captivity, God let him know that there was yet a long and eventful period of gentile world supremacy before Israel again gained her former glory and prominence.

Through a dream to Nebuchadnezzar which Daniel interpreted, and also through visions given to Daniel, God showed him the complete, long, war-ravished history of the gentiles down to the end of the time of the gentiles. The fulfillment of this advanced history in every detail has been one of the most astounding proofs of the immutability of the prophetical Scriptures. Skeptics and higher critics have freely attacked other portions of God's Word, but they wisely abstain from trying to explain away this prophecy. Either God gave a detailed history of the course of world events in advance, or if the Scriptures are not the Word of God, then man gave this advance history. There is no alternative explanation. To contribute this power to a mere man is too absurd for even the skeptics to advocate. As time transpired, world events and empires were molded into this advance pattern just as molten iron fills the pattern made in sand. This awesome demonstration of the foreknowledge of God is enough to convince any honest seeker after truth.

God used visual aid to simplify this advance history to Daniel. He gave a graphic picture of the future world empires in 'the form of a great statue resembling a man (Daniel 2:31-45) and also in a vision of four beasts. God showed the great colossus to Nebuchadnezzar in a dream, and when all the wise men of Babylon had failed to interpret the dream, God gave the interpretation to Daniel.

This image was a metallic image whose head was

gold, the breast and arms were silver, the abdomen was brass, the legs were iron, and the ten toes were part iron and part clay. The vision given to Daniel of four beasts represented the same empires as the great image and covered the same period of time. The vision of the four beasts was a supplement to the vision of the image and added some details. The first beast was like a lion with eagle's wings, the second was like a bear that raised up itself on one side, the third was like a leopard with four wings and four heads, and the fourth was diverse from all the others, dreadful and terrible with great iron teeth and ten horns.

God revealed to Daniel that the head of gold of the great image represented Nebuchadnezzar, or Babylon, the world empire in power at that time. The metals of this image decreased in value from the gold of the head down through the silver, the brass, and the iron and clay mixture of the toes. Nebuchadnezzar was an absolute monarch; he put to death whom he would and spared whom he would. The power of the rulers of the succeeding world empires was increasingly curbed by the aristocracy of Medo-Persia, the generals of Greece, the Senate of Rome, and finally by the parliaments of the democracies of the toes. The lion with the wings of an eagle of the beast vision represented the same empire and the same period of history as the head of gold of the image vision. The lion, the king of beasts, with the wings of an eagle, the king of birds, was a fitting emblem of the absolute monarchy that governed Babylon. Archaeologists have unearthed many magnificently sculptured lions with eagle's wings, which adorned the walls and gates of ancient Babylon as the national emblem.

God revealed to Daniel that following Babylon there would arise a world power represented by the two arms of the image vision and the bear that raised higher on one side of the beast vision. Here, God, by His wonderful foreknowledge, revealed a unique characteristic of the second world power that could hardly have been imagined, much less guessed, by human intellect. He revealed that the second world empire following Babylon would be a dual empire composed of two nations and that one would be more powerful than the other. It is a well-known historical fact that Medo-Persia fulfilled this prophecy and that the Persian power came up last and was more militaristic and stronger than Media. Our great God can even give details of the future. The bear of the beast vision had three ribs in its mouth. The three ribs, which the bear devoured, were Babylon, Lydia, and Egypt, which Medo-Persia conquered.

In this writing of the world history before it transpired, God depicted the empire that followed Medo-Persia by the abdomen of brass of the great image and the beast like a leopard with four heads of the beast vision. This empire has gone down in secular history as the Grecian Empire. God gave the leopard, one of the swiftest of beasts, as a fitting emblem of the swiftness of Alexander's conquests. He added emphasis to this swiftness by giving the leopard four wings. How could any human being who has ever lived have guessed that the small city states of the Greek peninsula without any form of central government could conquer the world in such a short time? Only God could have foreknown this.

The last world empire before the kingdom of heaven is set up on earth is symbolized by the legs of iron and feet part iron and part clay of the image seen in a dream by Nebuchadnezzar. The same empire is represented by the terrible fourth beast of Daniel's vision (Daniel 7:7) which had teeth of iron and ten horns on its head. The ten horns of the terrible beast correspond to the ten toes of the colossus. As all history students know, this fourth kingdom after Babylon that was strong as iron and subdued all others was Rome. Here God reveals that the form of the Roman Empire, when the times of the gentiles end, will be ten separate nations united in a confederacy. The book of Revelation deals principally with the last seven years of the times of the gentiles. This coincides with the last seven years of the Roman Empire in its ten-nation confederacy. Here is where many Bible students become confused.

Secular history considers the Roman Empire to have long since passed away, but not so with sacred history. Only the Caesars and what is known as Imperial Rome passed away about fifteen centuries ago.

TIMES OF THE GENTILES

The mighty ecclesiastical emperors of the powerful apostate church stepped on the throne of the political emperors without a break, and the power of Rome continued to rule supremely over most of the territory of the empire of the Caesars for another one thousand years. It has been only a little over four centuries since the power of the Roman pontiffs was relinquished over a small part of the empire, but over a large part of the empire the power of ecclesiastical Rome has continued without a break. It is true that in theory these toe nations of the empire have civil rulers, but these rulers cannot rule without the approval of the ecclesiastical power. The ecclesiastical Roman Empire operates in the political arena as political parties, under innocent sounding pseudonyms.

In Revelation 17, which deals with the last seven years of the times of the gentiles, we have some details revealed which God did not see necessary to reveal to Daniel. Verses 12 and 13 tell us that the ten horns of the beast are ten kings who shall reign as kings (rulers) one hour (short time) with the beast. Therefore, it is clear that the last stage of the Roman Empire will consist of a federation of at least ten nations ruled over by the Antichrist for a short time. It is proved in another chapter in this book that the woman riding the scarlet-colored beast, with a cup in her hand filled with the blood of saints and martyrs of Jesus, can be none other than ecclesiastical Rome. It is clearly shown in this seventeenth chapter of Revelation that Imperial Rome, revived for a short time in the form of a ten-nation confederacy, will uphold ecclesiastical Rome as the state religion and ecclesiastical Rome will be the central force that will revive the confederacy and hold it together for a short time.

This is exactly what is happening today within the confines of the geographical territory of the Roman Empire. Six nations within this territory have already confederated at a meeting of the heads of state held in Paris, and started the industrial wheels of the confederation rolling by eliminating trade barriers and pooling resources. The signs of the times are so clearly seen that even columnists of the daily press declare, "The dream of two thousand years is coming to pass: a United States of Europe." The coming into being of this United States of Europe makes us know that the times of the gentiles are coming to an end and the rapture is near. The Scriptures emphatically state that in the days of these kings the God of heaven shall set up a kingdom which shall never be destroyed (Daniel 2:44).

Why could this dream not come to pass in centuries gone by? Hannibal, Napoleon, the Kaiser, Hitler, and others dreamed and fought for this to come to pass. The immutable Scriptures declare that after Rome divides into the two divisions of the legs and later into the toe nations of the empire they will mingle themselves with the seed of men, but they will not cleave one to another, even as iron is not mixed with clay (Daniel 2:43). This Scripture has been fulfilled to every jot and tittle. Down through the centuries the royal rulers of these nations have intermarried, but have been fanatically nationalistic and have been almost continually at war among themselves. Something is happening among these toe nations today that has not happened for centuries. They claim to have learned that enmity among themselves is useless and they are determined to cleave together for security and economic advancement. For about fifteen centuries these toe nations have refused to cleave together, just as foretold in God's Word. It is foretold that in the very end of the times of the gentiles they will cleave together for a short time under one ruler (Revelation 17:12, 13). When this confederation is completely formed they consent to be ruled for a short time by a brilliant strategist, who will cause craft to prosper. This will be the ruler in power when Christ returns. These toe nations declare that the purpose of their uniting is to cause craft to prosper. It is predestined that the man who can do this will soon appear in their midst (Daniel 8:23-25). The Scriptures declare that soon after this man comes to power over these toe nations the Ancient of Days will sit in judgment, the Beast will be slain, and the saints of God shall possess the kingdom (Daniel 7:1-14, 21-27). The times of the gentiles will end and the literal kingdom of heaven will become an actuality. Just as the Scriptures declare, the wicked are doing wickedly and do not understand what is behind the tensions and convulsions of our time. It is hard for even the true Christian to grasp the nearness of the great tribulation and the kingdom of heaven soon to follow. Unbelief of the wicked and the inability of the Christians to grasp the meaning of the current events of our day will not stop the clock of prophecy one hour. According to the immutable Scriptures, "In the days of these kings" the kingdom of heaven will be set up. The beginning of the end of the times of the gentiles is already here.

CHAPTER VII

THE AGE OF THE CHURCH

> *And I say also unto thee, That thou art Peter, and upon this rock I will build my church; and the gates of hell shall not prevail against it.—Matthew 16:18.*
>
> *According as he hath chosen us in him before the foundation of the world, that we should be holy and without blame before him in love:—Ephesians 1:4.*

FROM the creation of man all through the antediluvian age and after the flood down to the call of Abraham, God dealt with the human race as one. The purpose of God in calling the Hebrew nation, later known as the Jews, was to choose a particular nation for His redemptive purpose. To this small segment of the race God gave His oracles and to them Christ was born to bless the entire race. From the call of Abraham to the Day of Pentecost God dealt with the human race in two divisions, Jew and gentile. During this period, God's particular attention and guidance was to the Jews as He developed His plan of salvation for the entire race of man through them.

On the first feast of Pentecost, after the resurrection of Christ, God created an entirely new thing —the church. This was a mystery hid in God, inasmuch as it was not revealed to former generations (Ephesians 3:2-6). The church was completely hidden from the Old Testament prophets. They prophesied that Christ would be a light to the gentiles and in Him the gentiles would trust (Amos 9:11, 12; Acts 15:16, 17), but it was not revealed to them that Christ would break down the middle wall of partition between Jews and gentiles and call out of the twain an entirely new body (Ephesians 2:14, 15).

The church is not formed by welding together the two divisions of the race, but is an organism composed of called-out ones from both Jews and gentiles. Although the church was hidden from men of other ages and is therefore known as a mystery, it was a well-known fact in the purpose of God. The church is not an afterthought of God, but was chosen in Him before the foundation of the world (Ephesians 1:4). Some contend that the church originated at the time God gave Israel the Law on Mt. Sinai. It is true that the word *church* is derived from *Ecclesia,* which means the called out of God. The Jews were called out from among the nations to be a separate people. In this sense, they might be called a church. Nevertheless, wherever the term *church* is used in the New Testament terminology it has no reference whatsoever to that division of the race known as Israelites, or Jews. This is clearly seen from the fact that the church was a mystery hidden during the Law Dispensation, or Jewish Dispensation. The fact that the Jews were a separate called-out people was anything but a mystery. Every ordinance and ritual that a Jew observed from the cradle to the grave taught him that he was called to be separate. Even at eight days of age all male Jews were circumcised as a sign they were set apart for God, separate from other people. The commandments, ordinances, and dietary laws constantly reminded the Jews that they were called to be a separate people. Therefore, they could not possibly be the church that was a mystery hidden from the ages before Christ.

The Church in Time

The church was yet future at the time of Christ's earthly ministry as Christ referred to it in the future tense. "Upon this rock I will build my church" (Matthew 16:18). At this time it was still a mystery (hidden in God), but Christ intimated that this mystery was soon to be revealed. Christ, during His earthly life, prepared the foundation of the church. He called, chose, and taught the apostles who were to be the foundation of the church, He Himself being the chief cornerstone (Ephesians 2:20). Here we have Christ shortly before His death referring to the church as yet future. Then a short time later after His ascension, we find the church referred to as being actually in existence (Acts 2:47). Therefore, the church was not formed by the Holy Ghost until the Day of Pentecost. Christ did not reveal the high standing of the church in the eternal councils of God, or the purpose of the church, or the form of government of the church. This was all revealed to Paul after the formation of the church. God also revealed that after sixty-nine weeks the Messiah would come and be cut off (crucified), but God did not reveal to Daniel and the Old Testament prophets the long parenthesis between the sixty-ninth and seventieth weeks.

During this parenthesis the entire church age has intervened. This is the period known in Holy Scriptures as the "fullness of the Gentiles" (Romans 11:25). At the close of the church age Israel will again occupy the center of the stage of prophecy and God will deal with the Jews directly as His grafted-in people again.

The Messages to Seven Churches

In this revelation to Daniel of the seventy weeks, in numerous other books in the Old Testament, and in Romans and Revelation of the New Testament God has given a detailed history of the seed of Abraham in advance, on out into the next age. In Daniel, Ezekiel, Revelation and other books God has given an advance history of the Gentiles. Prophecy would not be complete without an advance history of the church. If God did not give this history in Revelation 2 and 3, He did not give it at all; but that is just what our omniscient Creator did in these two chapters. Some contend that these messages are nothing more than a communication of God to seven local churches in Asia Minor and carry no prophetical significance. This view cannot stand up in the light of the Scriptures.

First, these messages are found in the book of Revelation. These messages are in an entirely different vein and style from the apostolic epistles, which were given for reproof, correction, instruction and edification. The first verse of the book expressly states that Christ's purpose here is to *show unto His servants things which must shortly come to pass. In* other words, things which were yet future. The remainder of the book is admitted by most commentators to be a revelation of future events. If these messages are ordinary pastoral letters, their setting is entirely out of context in this book of prophecy. The fact is that chapters 2 and 3 are in proper context and are prophetical in content just as the remainder of the book is prophetical. Christ tells John that the seven stars in His right hand are the angels of the seven churches and the candlesticks are the seven churches. There were many more local churches at this time besides the ones mentioned in these two chapters; they were just as important as the seven referred to here. The churches at Rome, Philippi, Colosse, Thessalonica, and Corinth were important enough to call for the immortal Epistles from the pen of Paul, the latter two having received two each. If these messages had only local significance as some proclaim, it would show the concern of Christ only for seven local churches to the neglect of the others. The fact that Christ stood in the midst of the candlesticks, which are the seven churches, and held the messengers of the seen churches in His right hand, shows that He, the Head of the church, will nurture, protect, and sustain His church down through the ages. These seven were representative churches which probably had in them conditions representative of the spiritual condition of seven stages of the church age.

The History of the Church

Ephesus

"Nevertheless I have somewhat against thee, because thou hast left thy first love" (Revelation 2:4).

The Ephesus Church was the first church period, the church of first love. The church of this period was nearer perfection than any of the periods to follow. This period saw Christianity at work in its purest form. This period had the light of the effulgent glory of the Son of God still lingering on earth from His earthly ministry. This period was blessed with the lives of the foundation stones of the church, the holy apostles, who had walked and talked with the Head of the church through His earthly ministry. Satan had not had time to sow the leaven of impurities in the meal of the glorious gospel as he has done in thousands of ways since. Christianity bloomed forth in all of its pristine, glorious majesty.

As lost mortal men collided with the gospel of life, it had a tremendous impact on their lives. To primitive Christians their religion was not a sideline or a social asset; it was life itself. Mortal man, dwelling in the shadow of death, had suddenly been translated from death unto life. They had not just found a philosophy of life, but they had found the source of life! The early Christians, with the fact of the resurrection of Christ fresh in their minds, were consumed with a desire to tell death-bound men that life and immortality had been brought to life. The fact of the resurrection had taken place in their lifetime! This glorious fact awed and possessed them; it had not had time to become commonplace to them as it has to our generation.

They were so convinced of the worthlessness of the riches and the pleasures of this world that they sold their possessions and lived as one family, welded together by divine love. They were nowhere commanded to practice community of wealth. This was a spontaneous action prompted by this new experience. On the other hand, they were commanded to have this fervent love (John 15:17). This divine love is the highest expression of a Christian experience. "God is love" (1 John 4:8). "By this shall all men know that ye are my disciples, if ye have love one to another" (John 13:35).

Men today have various unscriptural ideas of the manifestation of real Christianity. Some declare that material gain is a sign of real Christianity and God's favor. Some think popularity is a sign of deep spirituality and God's blessings. Others think that a self-proclamation of great power and gifts is a sign of spirituality and God's approval. Some use the self-created legend of possessing great powers for self-aggrandizement. Selfishness is the antithesis of divine love. The possession of divine love is declared to be more excellent than the possession of real gifts (1 Corinthians 12:31). The love of God is said to be the bond of perfection (Colossians 3:14). The ultimate achievement of an individual or a church is to reach the high plane where every act and desire is motivated by love.

Christ commended the Ephesus Church for their labor and patience, but He reproved them for leaving their first love. This was around A.D. 100 and the church had already slipped from the love of the early apostolic age. Christ warned that unless they repented and did their first works He would move the candlestick (lampstand) out of its place. The church, the lampstand or light holder for the heavenly light, would become useless if it degenerated to the place that its activities were motivated by anything except love for God and lost men. The history of the church from the Dark Ages until the present time has been

THE AGE OF THE CHURCH

recorded in cycles. Those groups that at first were humble and imbued with holy love for God and zeal for the salvation of the lost, had the divine honor of being the holder for the heavenly light of the gospel. As often as these groups became great in numbers and increased with material goods and lost their first love, God would choose a lesser, humble consecrated group for His candlestick. So has been the history of the church. The approximate date of this Ephesus period was from A.D. 30 to A.D. 170.

Smyrna

". . . Ye shall have tribulation ten days: be thou faithful unto death, and I will give thee a crown of life" (Revelation 2:10).

The second period of the church is outlined by a message addressed to Smyrna. *Smyrna* means "myrrh." Myrrh is a shrub which tastes bitter, but yields sweet perfume when crushed. The Smyrna Church was to be cast into prison and crushed by tribulation ten days. The overcomers were promised a crown of life if they were faithful unto death. This faithfulness, while being bruised by great persecution, yielded sweet incense before God. A day in Scripture does not always mean twelve hours or twenty-four hours. In many instances a day means a specific period of time.

The book of Revelation is a book of prophecy and the messages to the seven churches were mainly prophetical, portraying the history of the church. Just ten calendar days of persecution would not be significant enough to be noted in prophecy. These terrible ten days were ten periods of severe persecution by Imperial Rome. The history of these persecutions make one of the darkest annals in the history of the human race, being rivaled only by the persecution administered in later years by Ecclesiastical Rome. The Scriptures declare that this persecution would be instigated by the devil. Only the mind of the devil could have invented the diabolical tortures endured by the saints of this period. This was a determined effort of the enemy of righteousness to blot the church purchased by the blood of Jesus off the earth.

Satan invented the most excruciating methods of bringing death known in history. The faithful in Christ were skinned alive and salt sprinkled on the raw flesh. They were put on the rack and stretched until their joints were pulled apart. They were sawn asunder like sticks of wood. They were wrapped in skins of animals and thrown to wild dogs to be torn to shreds. Thousands and thousands were made human torches and burned to death. To read about these sufferings after 1900 years makes one shudder and at the same time thrill with admiration for the faith of the martyrs of this period.

One incident is especially notable: a child of God was asked by his fellow Christians to give a signal just before death by raising his hand to let them

THE AGE OF THE CHURCH

know if God was with him in this ordeal. As his Christian brethren stood on a hill afar off and watched, with the pungent odor of burning human flesh filling their nostrils, just before his soul was to take its flight to Paradise from a parched body, the martyr raised his hands to tell them God was still with him.

The historians of that day are critical of the bravery of the Christians and their desire for martyrdom. It is said that it seemed everyone the smoke touched became Christians. Of their own accord they came and confessed they were Christians. W h e n God makes up His jewels on the day when the trials of life are over and the redeemed rejoice in the light of God's face in the city which Christ has gone to prepare, we shall behold special crowns of life given to the martyrs of this Smyrna period. The bitter myrrh of the Smyrna period sent up a sweet incense before God which He will remember and reward on that day. The approximate date of the Smyrna Church is A.D. 170 to A.D. 312.

Pergamos

"But I have a few things against thee, because thou hast there them that hold the doctrine of Balaam, who taught Balac to cast a stumblingblock before the children of Israel, to eat things sacrificed unto idols, and to commit fornication. So hast thou also them that hold the doctrine of the Nicolaitanes, which thing I hate" (Revelation 2:14, 15).

It was said of the Pergamos Christians that they dwelled where Satan's seat is. The margin reads throne instead of seat. The city of Pergamos was at that time the headquarters or throne of Satan's religion. When the Babylonian Empire fell, the priests of the Babylonian cult fled to Pergamos in Asia Minor. Their descendants, the citizens of Pergamos, or the Pergamenes, built an assemblage of temples of idols to Zeus, Athene, Apollo, Aesculapius, Dionysus, Aphrodite. The most prominent Pergamene idol was Aesculapius. "The grove of Aesculapius was recognized by the Roman senate under Tiberius as having right of sanctuary. The serpent (Satan's image) was sacred to him, charms and incantations were among medical agencies then, and Aesculapius was called 'saviour' " (*Fausset's Bible Encyclopedia and Dictionary,* page 558).

Attalus, priest king of Pergamos, bequeathed his kingdom to Imperial Rome in 133 B.C. The emperors of Rome exercised the office of supreme pontiff of the Babylonian order until A.D. 376. At that time Gratian refused the office and in A.D. 378 Damasus, bishop of the church of Rome, was elected supreme pontiff of this cult. Therefore, through this scheme Satan managed to establish his throne over the apostate church of Rome. From this time pagan incantations, rituals and doctrines were mixed with a few Christian precepts in the church of Rome. The pure gospel story was adulterated with pagan doctrines and rituals and even the days that com-

THE AGE OF THE CHURCH

memorated great events in the history of Christianity were changed to conform to the dates and names prominent in paganism. It was in the Pergamos period that Satan managed to establish his throne over nominal Christianity.

Christ commended those that were faithful during this period for their work and for holding fast His name, but He reproved them for having the doctrine of Balaam and the doctrine of the Nicolaitanes. The doctrine of the Nicolaitanes will be discussed under the heading of the next church period. It is said to the Pergamos Church that they held the doctrine of Balaam, who taught Balac to cast a stumbling block before the children of Israel and to induce them to eat things sacrificed unto idols and to commit fornication. Balac, King of Moab, hired the prophet Balaam to curse the children of Israel. When the Lord refused to permit Balaam to curse them, Balaam devised a satanic scheme to invite the Israelites to the licentious feast of Moab. When the men of Israel came to the feast they committed fornication with the women of Moab and angered the Lord, who slew 24,000 Israelites.

Satan is very versatile. In the previous church age, he had tried to stamp out the true church by terrible persecution. One peculiarity of Christianity is that it thrives and stays pure under persecution. Satan suddenly reversed his tactics in the Pergamos age. The Emperor Constantine, in A.D. 312, proclaimed his conversion to Christianity. The persecutions suddenly stopped and the government favored Christianity and made it the state religion. Great government buildings were given to the Christians for houses of worship and the priests were clad in costly vestments. The church was enticed by Constantine's Balaamism to commit double fornication. Not only were the church and state united, but also pagan doctrines and rituals supplanted the pure gospel. From this time the church plunged into the dark night of the Thyatira period. Satan thus accomplished by favor, praise, and prosperity, what he could not do by persecution. The approximate date of the Pergamos age was from A.D. 312 to A.D. 600.

Thyatira

"Notwithstanding I have a few things against thee, because thou sufferest that woman Jezebel, which calleth herself a prophetess, to teach and to seduce my servants to commit fornication, and to eat things sacrificed unto idols" (Revelation 2:20).

The complaint the Lord had against the Thyatira Church was that it suffered a woman, Jezebel, who called herself a prophetess, to teach and seduce His servants to commit fornication and eat things sacrificed unto idols. The symbol of a woman in the Scripture typifies a religious economy. Israel is typified in Hosea by a woman. The true church is noted in the Scripture as a virgin espoused to one husband (2 Corinthians 11:2), who will be the bride at the marriage supper (John 3:29). In the parable of the leaven, it was a woman that hid the leaven in the meal of the true gospel.

This woman Jezebel of the Thyatira Church was a vile, notorious woman. She typified a church in a bad, ethical sense—the apostate church. Christ said He gave her space to repent of her fornication and she repented not; therefore, He would cast her into a bed and them that commit fornication with her into great tribulation (the great tribulation). Here is further proof that these messages go beyond the local churches addressed and are prophetical. If Jezebel were only a human female belonging to the local church at Thyatira, those who committed adultery with her could not have lived over 1900 years until the great tribulation. The meaning could not have been that the adulterers of that local church would be cast into tribulation during their lifetime and the true saints in the local church escape tribulation. The history of the church has proved just the opposite. It is the faithful ones who will not recant who receive persecution from the world. This woman was to continue through the ages and go into the tribulation. We see her again in Revelation 17 and find that it is the ten kings of the Antichrist's empire who turn against her and burn her flesh with fire, when she has attained the status of the state church of the Beast's empire, in the end of the age.

We see the beginning of this woman in the first church age, the Ephesus age. Here Christ said the "deeds" of the Nicolaitanes were in the church. A note in the Scofield Bible says Nicolaitanes is from *nikao,* "to conquer," and *laos,* "the people," or "laity." From this we see that there were those in the early church who wanted to divide an equal brotherhood and establish a priesthood and hierarchy patterned after the Levitical priesthood.

In the next age, the Pergamos Church age, the deeds had become a doctrine (Revelation 2:15). Constantine encouraged this doctrine and clothed the clergy in costly vestments that set them apart and gave them a conspicuousness in appearance. At the council of Nicaea in A.D. 325 the clergy emerged with more political power over the people. In Ephesus, it was deeds of the Nicolaitanes; in Pergamos it was a doctrine; and now in the Thyatira age it had developed into a fully organized church— Roman Catholicism.

The fornication of this woman consisted in the union of church and state and in the act of adulterating the pure gospel with all kinds of pagan "isms." The woman assumed the office of prophetess, when the bulls and the decrees of the pope began to supersede the Word of God. The Word of God was relegated to a minor importance and finally taken from the people. The doctrine of apostolic succession, the Immaculate Conception, purgatory, infant baptism, holy water, and many other heresies became articles of faith. Literal fornication was encouraged by a pseudo-celibacy of the priesthood and the sale of indulgences.

This woman Jezebel is to continue until the great tribulation. She received a curtailment of her world power by the Reformation, but she is rebounding in power in these last days before the tribulation. She has gained power until she can maneuver money from Protestant democracies to subsidize her schools and can keep cruel dictators on the throne in Catholic countries with Protestant money. Nevertheless, her days are short. She is predestined to use her political power to help consolidate the Beast Empire, but in the end the government of the Beast will turn against her and burn her flesh with fire. The approximate date of the Thyatira Church was A.D. 600 to A.D. 1517.

Sardis

"I know thy works, that thou hast a name that thou livest, and art dead" (Revelation 3:1).

"Thou hast a few names even in Sardis which have not defiled their garments; and they shall walk with me in white: for they are worthy" (Revelation 3:4).

If these messages are prophetical of seven consecutive stages of the church age, and the Thyatirian age was the dark age when the woman Jezebel (Roman Church) held sway, then the Sardis age of necessity would be the Reformation age. The Lord said that there were a few names in Sardis that had not defiled their garments and that they shall walk with Him in white for they are worthy. Those names, no doubt, were the reformers and saints who braved the wrath of the woman Jezebel (Roman Catholicism) to preach justification by faith.

None of these ages ended one day with the next age beginning the next day. These ages are not that sharply defined. The transition of one age to another cannot be relegated to one particular year. This transition period covered a number of years, during which time the conditions peculiar to the consecutive periods overlapped.

As the world was groping in darkness after more than one thousand years of the dark night of the reign of the Jezebel church, the mighty hand of God began to move to bring the light of the gospel back to the world. There were individual stars who began to shine in the dark sky of the pre-Reformation age such as John Wycliffe and John Huss. The reason for this spiritual darkness was that Rome had taken the Word of God from the people. This is the reason for the fanatical efforts put forth by Rome today to maintain separate schools: to keep the uncensored Word of God from her subjects. Where the uncensored Scriptures come in contact with the human mind, they enlighten and set free.

In preparing for the gospel light to shine again, God permitted Johann Gutenberg, in the fifteenth century, to invent movable type that made the printing press possible.

It has been said that the Reformation was possible because the mind of men came in direct contact with the Scripture. Then God put a hungering for righteousness into the heart of a young monk in Germany, Martin Luther. Luther, in his quest for righteousness that brings peace with God, secluded himself in a monastery. There he found a precious Bible and devoured its contents. Luther still tried to find peace of soul by self-punishment and observing the rituals and superstitions of the Roman Church. As his hunger for righteousness grew more intense, God spoke to him and brought to his mind that "the just shall live by faith." Luther immediately grasped and rejoiced in the light of the gospel and proclaimed the truth with boldness. He met and defeated the intellectual powers of Rome and defied her political and military might. Luther succeeded because this was the working of God. He has gone down in history as the guiding light of the Reformation, but there were others used of God to bring the gospel back to the world. In fact, Zwingli and Calvin broke more completely from the Roman superstitions and rituals than Luther did.

Ecclesiastical Rome immediately began a blood bath that equaled or even excelled Imperial Rome in letting the blood of believers. She partially filled the cup seen in her hand in Revelation 17 with the blood of the martyrs of Jesus at this time. The cup will be completely filled with the blood of Christians she will murder in the near future when she sits as queen and state church in the Beast's Empire. The Waldenses, Albigenses, Huguenots and thousands of others died at the hands of the Roman Church rather than give up their justification by faith. During this period, that woman Jezebel shed the blood of Christ's followers with such diabolical frenzy that it made Nero look morally good in comparison. Satan, by means of this wholesale slaughter, stopped the Reformation in Italy, France, Spain, Portugal, Ireland, and other countries. The gospel that sets free the soul also unshackles the mind. The countries that threw off the yoke of Rome prospered not only spiritually and in democratic liberty for the individual, but also in industrial development and scientific progress they outstripped and left behind those countries bound by the rule of Rome.

The Sardis period was said to have a name that they lived but were dead. They made a great step out of darkness but failed to get back to the first love. Justification by faith was rediscovered, but the blessed hope of the second coming, a Spirit-filled, Spirit-led life, and the millennial kingdom were not rediscovered. Bitter debates and differences were the order of the day instead of the unity and love of the early church. The Sardis period dates approximately from A.D. 1517 to about A.D. 1750.

Philadelphia

"I know thy works: behold, I have set before thee an open door, and no man can shut it" (Revelation 3:8).

"Because thou hast kept the word of my patience,

THE AGE OF THE CHURCH

I also will keep thee from the hour of temptation, which shall come upon all the world, to try them that dwell upon the earth" (Revelation 3:10).

The Lord said He had set before this church an open door. Some maintain this means the open door of the rapture. This could be possible, but there is a more plausible and scriptural interpretation. When Paul and Barnabas returned from their missionary journey to Antioch, they rehearsed to the church how God had opened the door of faith to the gentiles (Acts 14:27). Paul, speaking of his long and effective revival at Ephesus, said that a great door and effectual had been opened unto him (1 Corinthians 16:9). In Paul's request for prayer to the Colossians, he asked that they pray that God would open to him a door of utterance, to speak the mystery of Christ (Colossians 4:3). Since the middle of the eighteenth century, country after country has been opened to Christianity that previously was closed. There have been more evangelization and missionary work during this period than any other unless it was the first church age. The door has been opened in Africa, India, Japan, China, the Indies, and numerous islands of the sea. Only in the older civilized countries such as Italy, Spain, and Russia where Catholicism and Communism rule has the door to the gospel been practically closed.

This is another proof that the messages to the seven churches are prophetical. These seven churches were closely grouped in Asia Minor. One great power,

Rome, ruled the world at the time this revelation was given to John. The restraints and liberties affecting these churches were administered by this one power and affected all these churches alike. We know by authentic history that Rome did not give freedom to preach the gospel in Philadelphia alone and clamp down on the other churches. *Philadelphia* means "brotherly love." Although there have been periods of revival fervency and periods of declension during this Philadelphian age, in comparison to the Pergamean, Thyatirian, and Sardisian ages it has been a period of brotherly love and fellowship. One peculiarity has characterized this church age that did not stand out in other ages. One group or denomination would be honored with divine grace as the candlestick (light holder), but when they declined into worldliness and dead formality the candlestick would be moved to another group that would thirst for righteousness and tremble at God's word. T h e open door promised this church period most likely refers to the open door for the gospel that was opened to the Protestant countries by the Reformation and also the opening up of many heathen countries.

It is the consensus of most students of the Word that the Philadelphian age began about A.D. 1750. Because of one promise made to this church, there arises a difficult problem in determining the close of this age and the beginning of the Laodicean period. This promise is made in the following verse: "Because thou hast kept the word of my patience,

THE AGE OF THE CHURCH

I also will keep thee from the hour of temptation, which shall come upon all the world, to try them that dwell upon the earth" (Revelation 3:10). Most authors of books dealing with prophecy and the book of Revelation ignore this difficulty or gloss over it in a contradictory manner. It seems that there is a hesitancy on the part of authors in admitting that there are some things not clearly revealed as yet. It seems that there is a tendency to think that an author of a work on prophecy should be an infallible authority and never admit that there are some as yet unknown factors. They seem to think that an admission like this would lower the prestige of their composition.

To the contrary, the proclamation that one person has a full revelation of all the prophetical Scriptures is looked on with skepticism by those well versed in the Scriptures. Daniel, the man to whom God gave the most astounding prophetical revelations of any man in the ages before Christ, did not have all the answers. God showed him the history of His people (the Jews) down to the millennium and a detailed history of the gentile world powers down to the time the literal kingdom of heaven would be set up. God even revealed to him the number of days between the momentous events at the very close of this age. God revealed that from the time the Beast placed his image in the temple and demanded that the world worship him, there would be 1,290 days until a momentous event. Then God added 45 more days before another great event in the history of the world. It is easy for us to deduce that these events concern the sweeping away of the debris of the shattered gentile world power and the assumption by Christ of the throne of David and the time of the beginning of the millennium.

God did not tell Daniel plainly what these momentous events were. Daniel's spiritual appetite was whetted to know all the details. "O my Lord, what shall be the end of these things?" (Daniel 12:8). God, as a solicitous father to His inquiring child, tells Daniel the words are closed up and sealed until the time of the end, and assures him that he will be resurrected and stand in his lot at the end of the days and be a joyous spectator of the events that had been withheld from him. God did not give even Daniel all of the answers. God does not reveal many exact dates to man, but lets us know when they are near, even at the door.

It is agreed by most students of Scripture that the "hour of temptation" that the Philadelphia Church is to be kept from is the great tribulation during the last week of gentile dominion before the kingdom of heaven is set up on earth. It is a clear fact taught in the Scriptures that the reason the saints will be kept from the great tribulation is because they will be raptured. "For the Lord himself shall descend from heaven with a shout, with the voice of the archangel, and with the trump of God: and the dead in Christ shall rise first: then we which are alive and remain shall be caught up together with them in the clouds, to meet the Lord in the air: and so shall we ever be with the Lord" (1 Thessalonians 4:16, 17). "Behold, I show you a mystery; We shall not all sleep, but we shall all be changed, in a moment, in a twinkling of an eye, at the last trump: for the trumpet shall sound, and the dead shall be raised incorruptible, and we shall be changed" (1 Corinthians 15:51, 52).

Most expositors hold that the rapture closes the church age. Therefore, if the rapture closes the church age and it takes place in the Philadelphian age, this leaves no place for the Laodicean Church unless it goes out into the tribulation. Many expositors of renown proclaim that this can never happen: that Christ's body is not divisible and if some members go in the rapture all will go. They seem to forget that these messages are prophetical and that they do not deal exclusively with Christ's body, the living organism made up of lively numbers who are daily receiving spiritual life and nourishment from the head of the body. These messages deal with the mystery form of the kingdom of heaven in its broadest sense, the sphere of profession. In most of these messages, Christ warns those who are in grave error and heresy. In the Thyatirian Church He deals with the vile woman Jezebel, the apostate church of the Dark Ages. So we see it is the sphere of Christian profession dealt with in Revelation 2 and 3.

We also see this truth brought out in the parable where the net is cast into the sea and is filled with both good and bad fish. Of course, the true body is within the bounds of this sphere of profession. Christ makes special promises of rewards to the faithful in all these periods. Christ tells the Laodicean Church that He will spew it out of His mouth. He will not spew the true Spirit-filled saints out of His mouth at His coming, but they will be raptured. Therefore, He could not be speaking in these messages exclusively to the true church.

We also have the revelation in Matthew 25 where the kingdom of heaven is likened unto ten virgins; five were wise and had oil, but five were foolish and their oil had leaked out. The wise went into the marriage, but the foolish were left out. This sounds very much like the Laodiceans whom Christ spews out of His mouth. Some expositors have gone far enough to declare that this Scripture concerning the ten virgins is just simple narrative and has no spiritual significance. If we are honest seekers of truth, we cannot read out of these Scriptures the emphatic statement *the kingdom of heaven is likened unto ten virgins.* If this parable is just so many words and has no spiritual meaning, how can one be consistent and teach that the other parables have any meaning? Is it not irreverent to teach that part of Christ's words were idle words without meaning? Christ said, "The words that I speak unto you, they are spirit, and they are life," John 6:63. We do know that there is a great multitude out of every nation saved during the tribulation; they are killed by the Beast for their testimony (Revelation 7:9-14). Who could we believe would be more apt to realize what they had missed in the rapture and understand the awful significance of the mark of the Beast than those who had had some connection with the sphere of Christian profession? These seem to have points of similarity to the foolish virgins who went to buy oil. The writer does not intend to be dogmatic in this belief, but it seems to have a scriptural basis.

All the difficulty arises from the statement "I also will keep thee from the hour of temptation." This promise is made to the Philadelphian Church. The Laodicean, or seventh church, is the next one addressed. If the promise had been made to the Laodicean Church, there would be no difficulty: the rapture would close the last church age, which is logical. Some students of Scripture proclaim that the promise is to the Philadelphian saints—the brotherly love ones, Spirit-filled, with zeal for souls in the Laodicean period—who will be kept from the tribulation by means of the rapture, which will end the church ages. Whatever the true interpretation is, we do know that Christ will return before the great tribulation and catch away those who are ready. We do not have to depend on the prophecy in Revelation 2 and 3 concerning the church age to prove that the second coming is imminent. The Scriptures that deal directly with the events of the end of the age have had ample fulfillment to prove that the second coming is near. The current events, which are the fulfillment of the prophetical Scriptures dealt with in previous chapters, could not possibly be accidental, but are irrefutable assurance that the second coming of Christ is near. The Scriptures that deal directly with the events of the end of the age have had ample fulfillment to prove this.

Laodicean Period

"I know thy works, that thou art neither cold nor hot: I would thou wert cold or hot. So then because thou art lukewarm, and neither cold nor hot, I will spew thee out of my mouth" (Revelation 3:15, 16).

This is the last church addressed in these messages. It must be remembered that we cannot confine the transition of these ages from one phase to another to a certain year or even a certain decade. The conditions that are prominent in the first part of one age begin to prevail in the last years of the preceding age. The conditions today seem to be almost more Laodicean than Philadelphian. It is said that this church is lukewarm. That is an apt description of most of the sphere of Christian profession today.

In most churches today the spiritual atmosphere is hardly lukewarm. The fervency and simplicity of a generation ago are gone. The worship services are carried on in a sedate ritualistic manner; the expression of spiritual joy and a personal fellowship with

God is a rarity. Many local churches are no more than social clubs concerned with halfhearted efforts to reform the world. They have lost sight of the fact that the church is supposed to be the light holder of the gospel which makes new creatures of those called out of the world. Many churches have become merely the community center for social activities. That part of the program of the church that is not given to social activities is taken up with committees, societies, bands, clubs and boards. Evangelistic efforts are mainly mechanical and directed toward "churching" the "unchurched." Many proclaim we are in the midst of a national revival and point to the great increase in church membership as evidence. It may truthfully be said that a revival works a moral revolution in an individual or a community. Some of the most highly publicized revivals today hardly create a moral ripple on the sea of humanity.

The Laodicean Church says of itself that it is increased with goods and has need of nothing; and knowest not that it is wretched, miserable, poor, blind, and naked. If magnificent, costly edifices would save the race, it would already be saved today. Never before have churches been so well off in material things as now, but in spiritual things they are wretched and poor and blind. One pastor has been praised for having the ingenuity to invent a revolving pulpit that can be used for religious services and then be turned around and thereby convert the sanctuary into a dance hall.

The materialistic mania has so gripped the sphere of the profession called the church that they inject the promise of material gain into their efforts to "church" people. People are being taught if they will acknowledge God and participate in church activities, they will have success in their business efforts. The idea that people can use God to gain their desires is being used as an incentive to embrace religion. This error has progressed so far that it is common for a prize fighter, after he has mauled his opponent into a bloody pulp, to immediately and dramatically thank God for helping in the bloody work. This error is being taught by many instead of the truth that a person has to deny himself and consecrate his life to the extent that God can use him in order to obtain salvation.

Instead of the erroneous theory that the church will gradually convert the world, the Scriptures teach that the sphere of Christian profession will completely apostatize in the end of the church age. "This know also, that in the last days perilous times shall come. For men shall be lovers of their own selves, covetous, boasters, proud, blasphemers, disobedient to parents, unthankful, unholy, without natural affection, trucebreakers, false accusers, incontinent, fierce, despisers of those that are good, traitors, heady, highminded, lovers of pleasure more than lovers of God; having a form of godliness, but denying the power thereof: from such turn away" (2 Timothy 3:1-5). "For the time will come when they

THE AGE OF THE CHURCH

will not endure sound doctrine; but after their own lusts shall they heap to themselves teachers, having itching ears; and they shall turn away their ears from the truth, and shall be turned unto fables" (2 Timothy 4:3, 4).

Church history for over 1900 years has been shaped according to this prophetic mold in Revelation 2 and 3. According to this prophetic mold the church age is near an end and the second coming of Christ is near. It is time for the faithful in Christ to renew their consecration and to look up, for their redemption draweth nigh.

CHAPTER VIII

WHEN DUST SHALL SING

> *And many of them that sleep in the dust of the earth shall awake, some to everlasting life, and some to shame and everlasting contempt.* —Daniel 12:2
>
> *Thy dead men shall live, together with my dead body shall they arise. Awake and sing, ye that dwell in dust: for thy dew is as the dew of herbs, and the earth shall cast out the dead.* —Isaiah 26:19.

THROUGH Adam, death passed upon all men. Death has stalked the human race from Adam until now, and will continue to reign until the end of the millennial kingdom. Until Jesus Christ conquered death, men were all their lifetime subject to bondage through the fear of death (Hebrews 2:15). The agonizing scenes of a parent watching the gasping breath of a beloved child, or a child watching a parent die and pass into the unknown have happened billions of times since Abel's death saddened the hearts of Adam and Eve. The sorrow of death has blighted every home that ever existed in past generations. The whole human race grasped, hoped, and yearned for the answer to what is beyond death as they beheld death reap generation after generation. The burning question that had occupied the last thoughts of dying millions was framed in words when Job asked, "If a man die, shall he live again?" (Job 14:14). On that most glorious day of all human ages, when Christ stepped alive from a borrowed tomb and proclaimed, "I am alive for evermore," He answered this question for the entire race. To those who receive Him, Christ proclaims, "Because I live, ye shall live also."

The Meaning of Death

To understand what takes place at death, one has to understand the nature of man as revealed by the Scriptures. The Scriptures reveal that man is a trinity—body, soul, and spirit. "I pray God your whole spirit and soul and body be preserved blameless unto the coming of our Lord Jesus Christ" (1 Thessalonians 5:23). "The word of God is quick, and powerful, and sharper than any twoedged sword, piercing even to the dividing asunder of the soul and spirit . . ." (Hebrews 4:12). Because man has a body, he is world-conscious; that is, he, through the five senses of the body, has contact with his physical environment. The senses by which man contacts the material world are sight, hearing, smell, taste, and feeling. The seat of the appetites and fleshly desires is in the body. Those who are carnal and live to satisfy these desires never rise above the animal plane of life regardless of their culture or wealth.

Because man is a soul, he is self-conscious; he is conscious of being a separate entity from all others. The soul is the seat of the conscience, affections, and emotions.

Because man is a spirit, he is God-conscious and can have communion with God, who is spirit. In unregenerate man, the spirit is in what might be called a dormant state. This condition necessitates a spiritual awakening or regeneration before man can enjoy spiritual things. Jesus called this recreating work of God a new birth.

When the soul and spirit move out of the body, death of the body takes place. Death is not cessation of life; the soul does not even sleep or become unconscious at death. The Scriptures clearly teach that death is only a moving out of the soul and spirit from the body. Paul called the body in which the conscious man lives simply a house or a tabernacle. "For we know that if our earthly house of this tabernacle were dissolved, we have a building of God, an house not made with hands, eternal in the heavens" (2 Corinthians 5:1). "Therefore we are always confident, knowing that, whilst we are at home in the body, we are absent from the Lord: (for we walk by faith, not by sight:) we are confident, I say, and willing rather to be absent from the body, and to be present with the Lord" (2 Corinthians 5:6-8).

Paul continues to teach the separation of the soul and body when he said he knew a man (Paul) who was caught up to the third heaven into paradise. He states that he did not know if this man was in the body or out of the body (2 Corinthians 12:1-4). Probably Paul was out of the body, for he said this happened "above fourteen years ago." According to Usher's Chronology, fifteen years before this time they stoned Paul at Lystra and dragged him out of the city, thinking him to be dead. His enemies thought him dead for keeps, but God let His faithful servant take a short vacation in paradise.

In the episode of the rich man and Lazarus, we see that their souls were conscious and could feel, talk, hear, remember, and express concern for others after they left the body in death. They could even recognize each other in their soulish body. Also, the souls of the tribulation saints, who were slain by the Beast, could talk, remember, wear robes, and desire justice. The relating of a death episode in the Old Testament teaches plainly that death is only a moving out of the soul. When the son of the woman who fed Elijah at Zarephath died and Elijah besought the Lord to make him alive again, he prayed in this manner, "O Lord my God, I pray thee, let this child's soul come into him again" (1 Kings 17:21). The Lord heard Elijah, and when the soul came back into the dead body, the child was alive again. Those sinners who try to defeat the justice of God by having their bodies cremated and their ashes sprinkled upon the waters do not understand the nature of their own existence. Sinners are already in punishment before the body is cremated.

The Habitation of Departed Souls Before the Resurrection of Christ

From the first death in the human family until the resurrection of Christ, all souls, both saved and lost, went to Sheol, or Hades, in the heart of the earth. The saved were separated from the lost by a great gulf (Luke 16:26). The compartment of Hades, where the saved were comforted, was known as Abraham's bosom, or paradise. The Greek noun *Hades* is translated *hell* in English. The word *hell* as it is used today designates the compartment of Hades where the lost are punished. We must remember that Hades, before Christ's resurrection, included both the abode of the saved and lost. This place of departed spirits is known in Hebrew as Sheol.

Christ Himself tells us that Hades is in the heart of the earth. He told the Pharisees that He was going to the heart of the earth (Matthew 12:40). He told the penitent thief that He and the thief were going that very day to paradise (Luke 23:43). Therefore, paradise at that time was in the heart of the earth. There are those who try to deny punishment for the wicked after death by claiming that Sheol and Hades should be translated grave. They give as proof the statement that Jacob made that he would go down to Sheol mourning for Joseph (Genesis 37:35). Their interpretation is that Jacob was a saved man, and if he were going to Sheol, he was going to the grave and not a place of punishment. Jacob only meant he would go down to Abraham's bosom or paradise at death. There are other Scriptures that substantiate the fact that all departed spirits, before Christ's resurrection, went to Hades in the heart of the earth. The earth opened up and Korah went down alive into hell or Sheol (Numbers 16:33). "Though they dig into hell, thence shall mine hand take them" (Amos 9:2). The Scriptures also refer to hell as being beneath.

Paradise Changed

At the time of the resurrection of Christ, paradise was changed from below into the third heaven. Many students of the Scripture who linger and rejoice over Isaiah 53:5, which tells us He was wounded for our transgressions, bruised for our iniquities, chastised for our peace, and striped for our healing, fail to see another great work of Christ at His first advent. One of the most glorious prophecies in the Old Testament concerning the work of Christ at His first advent was that He would bring out the prisoners from the prison house (Isaiah 42:7). The preceding verse (Isaiah 42:6) connects this with His first advent when He would be given as a covenant of the people and for a light of the gentiles.

Who were these prisoners? In Zechariah 9:9 where it was foretold that Christ would ride the colt into Jerusalem, the following verses refer to these prisoners as *thy* prisoners and also prisoners of hope. "As for thee also, by the blood of thy covenant I have sent forth thy prisoners out of the pit wherein is no water. Turn you to the strong hold, ye prisoners of hope: even to day do I declare that I will render double unto thee" (Zechariah 9:11, 12). The prisoners of hope were the righteous dead from Abel down to the resurrection of Christ. It is said of Satan that he opened not the house of his prisoners (Isaiah 14:17). This has reference to the lost on the opposite side of Hades, across the gulf from paradise.

Job, in the dark hours of his suffering and despondency, lamented the fact that he had ever been born and refers to the souls in paradise as prisoners. "Why died I not from the womb? why did I not give up the ghost when I came out of the belly? . . . Or as an hidden untimely birth I had not been; as infants which never saw light. There the wicked cease from troubling; and there the weary be at rest. There the prisoners rest together; they hear not the voice of the oppressor" (Job 3:11, 16-18).

These prisoners of hope in paradise below were delivered when Christ arose. It is stated that "the graves were opened; and many bodies of the saints which slept arose, and came out of the graves after his resurrection" (Matthew 27:52, 53). Paul, in regard to this event, said, "When he ascended up on high, he led captivity captive, and gave gifts unto men. (Now that he ascended, what is it but that he also descended first into the lower parts of the earth?

. . .)" (Ephesians 4:8, 9).

Christ had told the penitent thief that the place into which He would descend in the lower part of the earth would be paradise. When He ascended up on high He changed paradise to the third heaven. In later years, Paul said he was caught up into the third heaven into paradise (2 Corinthians 12:2-4). This is what Christ meant when He said the gates of hell (Sheol) would not prevail against His Church. Many sermons have been preached on the thesis that no power or persecution will ever prevail against His Church. Imperial Rome and the Roman Church have both prevailed against the true Church. Multiplied millions of Christians have been slain by the enemies of Christ's Church, but the gates of hell or Sheol have never prevailed against the New Testament Church. All the righteous dead from Christ's resurrection until now have at death been carried up to the third heaven into paradise.

When Jesus of Nazareth stepped from Joseph's tomb that most glorious day earth has ever witnessed, He shook three worlds: the spirit world, the world of mortal men, and the world of the righteous dead. The spirit world of angels was moved with awe and adoration because of the manifestation of the power and love of God. The spirit world of wickedness was silenced and subdued because their prince was judged and defeated and their greatest victory had now become their greatest defeat. A new dawn had arisen on the world of mortal men because salvation from sin had been purchased, death had been conquered, life and immortality had been brought to light. The world of righteous dead, who had dwelt in Abraham's bosom below as prisoners of hope, was thrilled with ecstasy when the risen Christ led captivity captive and changed Paradise from below to above.

The Order of the Resurrection

"For as in Adam all die, even so in Christ shall all be made alive. But every man in his own order: Christ the firstfruits; afterward they that are Christ's at his coming" (1 Corinthians 15:22, 23). The glorious doctrine of the resurrection of man was more or less latent in the Old Testament. It remained for the New Testament to reveal this truth in all its glory and establish it as an anchor for the souls of mortal men. In the Old Testament the resurrection was taught by implication and in some instances directly. A few Old Testament characters such as Job, Daniel, and Isaiah received a direct revelation of the resurrection. During the 400 years between Malachi and Christ, the Jews digested the prophets and the doctrine of the resurrection became more prominent, until at the time of Christ the resurrection had emerged as a fundamental doctrine of the sect of the Pharisees, the largest religious group of the Jews. The truth of the resurrection became the very center, the foundation stone, of the Christian religion. The gospel can be summed up in one sentence: Christ arose from the dead and because He lives those who believe on Him can live also.

Paul declares, "For as in Adam all die, even so in Christ shall all be made alive. But every man in his own order: Christ the firstfruits; afterward they that are Christ's at his coming. Then cometh the end . . ." (1 Corinthians 15:22-24). This order of the resurrection was implied in the order of the Jewish harvest. They were instructed to gather the first ripe grain and give a wave offering to the Lord. Then came the main harvest, and after the main harvest the gleaning. The New Testament reveals that the wave offering was a type of Christ who became the firstfruits of the first resurrection. Christ and a number of the Old Testament saints who arose with Him were typified by this wave offering.

At the second coming of Christ the dead in Christ will arise and the living saints will be changed in a moment, in the twinkling of an eye. This will constitute the main harvest of the first resurrection. "For the Lord himself shall descend from heaven with a shout, with the voice of the archangel, and with the trump of God: and the dead in Christ shall rise first: then we which are alive and remain shall be caught up together with them in the clouds, to meet the Lord in the air: and so shall we ever be with the Lord" (1 Thessalonians 4:16, 17). The main harvest of the first resurrection will take place at the first phase of the second coming of Christ.

Then the great tribulation convenes on earth under the reign of the Beast. During this great tribulation a great multitude will refuse to worship the ruler of the United Nations of Europe (Revived Rome) and to receive his mark. Because of their faith in Christ, they will be killed by the Beast. In Revelation 6 we see a glimpse of the souls of these tribulation saints. At the end of the great tribulation they will be resurrected and become the gleanings of the first resurrection (Revelation 20:4).

In Revelation 20:5, 6 the resurrection of the righteous is referred to twice as the first resurrection. In years gone by most persons believed the resurrection of the righteous and the resurrection of the lost would take place at the same time. The Scriptures emphatically teach that these resurrections are separated by one thousand years. This one-thousand-year period is known as the millennium, during which Satan is bound and Christ reigns on earth. The order of the resurrection is: Christ the first fruits, then the first resurrection at Christ's second coming, then the great tribulation at the end of which the tribulation saints will be resurrected. Next in order is the one-thousand-year reign, "then cometh the end" (end of the millennium) when the white-throne judgment takes place and the wicked dead are raised and judged. Christ foretold the resurrection of life and the resurrection of damnation in the same sentence; nevertheless, other Scriptures reveal the one thousand years between these two resurrections (Revelation 20:5).

Some have asked in confusion if the wicked at death go to the compartment of Hades where the wicked are punished, why does God resurrect and judge them and cast them back into hell? The Scriptures do not teach this. Hell gives up the wicked and they are judged and cast into the lake of fire at the end of the millennium. Satan, his angels, and lost men are cast into the lake of fire at the close of the millennium. As has been stated, hell is a translation of the Greek word *Hades*. The lake of fire is derived from *Gehenna*. These are two separate, distinct places. Hell is the jail or abode of the wicked until trial or judgment, then the eternal sentence is to the lake of fire. This is the second death.

The Resurrected Body

The glorious, resurrected, immortal body is beyond description. The Scriptures declare that it will be like the Lord's own glorious body (Philippians 3:21). That body was flesh, bone, and spirit; yet He could pass through closed doors at will. Christ after His resurrection had the same features and the nail scars in His hands. That body was so real that He ate fish and honeycomb to prove His reality. The resurrection body is free from sickness and infirmities and is not subject to the law of gravity. The intellect and capacity to enjoy God's presence and wonderful creation will be infinitely increased. Now we know in part, but then we shall know even as we are known. The greatest achievement that can ever be reached by mortal man is to know Christ and have the assurance that when He shall appear, we shall be like Him, for we shall see Him as He is.

That monster, death, the greatest enemy of man, has stilled the voice of the billions who have passed across the stage of this earth. Multiplied millions have learned to enjoy God's beautiful creation and have expressed their joy in music, poetry, and song; but their tongues have been stilled by death. Millions of husbands and wives, who have known the thrill of love in their youth, then shared the joy and disappointments of life together, and then in old age when the bonds of union have grown stronger than ever, have had the voice of their beloved companion stilled by the monster death. Millions of young brides and bridegrooms have had the voice of their companions suddenly stilled by death. Millions of parents have felt the warmth of little arms around their necks and thrilled to the prattle of a baby's cooing voice only to have that voice stilled by death. It is a glorious thought to know that these voices were not stilled forever, but those who were redeemed will sing again.

The visitors in the catacombs of Rome can view the subterranean tombs where thousands of saints of God lived and died in hope of the resurrection. All that remains of these soldiers of the cross to be seen by pious pilgrims today is the dust of the tabernacles that once housed their immortal souls. The voices that once praised God in psalms and hymns and spiritual songs are stilled today, but they shall sing again. The tongues of millions, since apostolic days who sang as they wended their way through this world as strangers and pilgrims looking for a heavenly country, have had their voices that sang praises with joy stilled by death; but those voices shall sing again.

The mother of the writer, who sang as her hands tilled the stubborn hills of the southern Appalachians so that her children might eat, shall sing again. As the writer enjoys the reminiscence of childhood in the majestic Smoky Mountains, where freedom was enjoyed more than it is anywhere in America today, he can recall pleasant, carefree, beautiful scenes. Even the animals reveled in freedom and the horses, cows, and sheep were not imprisoned by fences. The milch cows wore large bells which gave out clear, resonant tones that seemed to blend with the bark of the squirrel, the dirge of the whippoorwill, and the fragrance of the rhododendron. Sometimes the cows would not come home at night for milking. The writer can remember trotting along beside a mountain mother who knew the real origin of species, and would answer every inquiry of a young mind about the beauties of nature with a "God made it that way." At intervals, that mother would cup her hand to her ear and listen for the familiar ding dong of the cow's bell. Sometimes her voice would ring out clear as the cowbell and reverberate from hill to beautiful hill with the lines of the wonderful old hymn:

WHEN DUST SHALL SING

How tedious and tasteless the hours
  When Jesus no longer I see!
Sweet prospects, sweet birds, and sweet flow'rs
  Have all lost their sweetness for me

The midsummer sun shines but dim;
  The fields strive in vain to look gay;
But when I am happy in Him,
  December's as pleasant as May.

The hills are still there, but they are not the paradise of freedom as they once were. The mountaineers were forced to leave their beloved hills so that a national park might be provided for thousands of others to behold the beauties of God's handiwork. The beautiful tones of the cowbells are heard reverberating among the hills no more. The writer returns to a country cemetery in the hills of Tennessee and stands in the twilight at the hour the cows should be coming home and tries to recapture some of his childhood. As he listens, there are no strains of "How tedious and tasteless the hours when Jesus no longer I see"; only the whine of the wind in the cedars and the lonesome cooing of the turtle dove. The vocal chords which sang so clearly and sweetly, "but when I am happy in Him, December's as pleasant as May" are returned to dust, but that dust shall sing again. This fact was made certain for all time, when Jesus of Nazareth, God's Son, stepped from Joseph's tomb and said, "I am alive forever more and have the keys of hell and death." "Because I live, you can live also."

The feeling of the writer is expressed in the lines of an old hymn:

If I should be living when Jesus comes,
  And know the day and the hour,
I'd like to be standing at mother's tomb
  When Jesus comes in His power.
I'd like to say "Mother, this is your boy,
  You left when you went away;
And now my dear mother it gives me great joy
  To see you again today."

If the songs of the redeemed pilgrims are sweet as they pass through this short life praising God for redeeming love, how sweet shall be the song of those whose bodies have arisen from the dust, free from mortality, and are pulsating with eternal life? Yes, many that sleep in the dust shall awake, Daniel 12:2. The earth shall cast out her dead, the silent dust shall sing again , Isaiah 26:19.

CHAPTER IX

WHEN MEN SEEK DEATH

> *And in those days shall men seek death, and shall not find it; and shall desire to die, and death shall flee from them.*
> —Revelation 9:6.

THE human race is yet to experience the most eventful and awful week of its entire existence. In view of the fulfillment of prophecy, this terrible week of seven years is near at hand. This time of trouble is known in the Scripture as the great tribulation. Jeremiah calls this tribulation the time of "Jacob's trouble" (Jeremiah 30:7). Ezekiel calls it a "furnace" for melting Israel (Ezekiel 22:19-22). Daniel calls it a "time of trouble" (Daniel 12:1). Joel calls it "a day of darkness and of gloominess" (Joel 2:2). Jesus said there had not been so great tribulation from the beginning of the world, no, nor ever shall be (Matthew 24:21, 22). Jesus warns His people to watch and pray always that they may be able to escape this tribulation (Luke 21:36). The book of Revelation describes the great tribulation in detail.

In the astounding revelation given to Daniel depicting the future history of Israel, God divides this future history into three divisions: seven weeks, sixty-two weeks, and one week. World history has proved that these weeks are weeks of seven years each. In seven weeks plus sixty-two weeks, from the commandment to r e s t o r e and build Jerusalem, Messiah was to come and be cut off (crucified). These sixty-nine weeks were fulfilled at the crucifixion of Christ; this leaves one week of seven years for Israel to be dealt with before everlasting righteousness in the form of the kingdom of heaven shall be brought in.

Unknown to the Old Testament prophets, but hidden in God, was the mystery of the church, which was destined to come in between the sixty-ninth and seventieth week. When Christ came, the Jews crucified the King from heaven and were broken off through unbelief. During this parenthesis between the sixty-ninth and seventieth week, the gentiles have been grafted into favor with God through faith. There remains this one week in the future for God to deal directly with Israel and bring the Jews to repentance and conversion.

Without controversy, this will be earth's most momentous week. This week will end the times of the gentiles and cause the conversion of the Jews; it will finish the transgression, make an end of sins, make reconciliation for iniquity, bring in everlasting righteousness, seal up the vision and prophecy, and at its close the most Holy will be anointed as King on David's throne here on earth (Daniel 9:24).

This week will be the transition between two of the world's greatest ages; it will see the whole world order changed. The events of this week will change the kingdoms of this world into the kingdom of heaven. All forms of government, such as democracies, monarchies, and dictatorships, will be superseded by a world-wide theocracy. It will be a time of the greatest suffering and catastrophe the race has ever known.

During this seven years the Antichrist will rule over a confederation of nations within the territory of Imperial Rome. The Scriptures consider this the last stage of the Roman Empire. This does not exclude the influence of the Antichrist over other nations outside this territory by means of treaties, alliances, and pacts. The center of the Antichrist government will be within the territory of the Roman Empire, but the great tribulation will affect to a great extent the whole world.

The Scriptures make it plain that the nations of the East with their millions, as well as Revived Rome, will march to Palestine for this last great conflict (Revelation 16:12-14). It is not clear whether these nations of the East will march to Palestine as satellites of Magog (Russia) or at the call of the Antichrist; nevertheless, they will be there for the slaughter. Many of the alliances and power blocks that are forming today are shaping the nations into the positions they will occupy at the time of the great tribulation. Many discerning Bible students today can see the storm clouds of the tribulation already gathering and casting their shadows upon this troubled, perplexed world.

Many passages of Scripture in the Old Testament give glimpses of the great tribulation, but the major portion of the book of Revelation is concerned with the great tribulation. From the sixth through the nineteenth chapter of Revelation we are given details of the great tribulation, many of which are not given in any other book of the Bible. The book is highly symbolical. The judgments of the tribulation are given under the symbols of seven seals, seven trumpets, and seven vials. There are many parentheses in the description of these judgments which portray individuals, groups, and institutions prominent during the tribulation.

From Revelation 1 to Revelation 6 the scene is filled with the giving of the revelation on the Isle of Patmos, the church ages, and the scene in heaven. In chapter 6, Christ begins to break the seals out of which proceed the events of the great tribulation.

The First Seal

"And I saw, and behold a white horse: and he that sat on him had a bow; and a crown was given unto him: and he went forth conquering, and to conquer," Revelation 6:2.

Out of the first seal proceeded a rider on a white

horse with a bow in his hand; a crown was given unto him and he went forth conquering and to conquer. This rider going forth to conquer is not Christ, as is supposed by some; neither does he represent the gospel. Christ came to bring salvation and the gospel began to go forth nearly two thousand years before this event symbolized here. This is none other than the notorious person who occupies such an important place in both the Old and New Testaments, who will rule over the confederacy of Revived Rome in the last week of this gentile age. In Daniel he is known as the "Little Horn," in 2 Thessalonians as the "Man of Sin," in Revelation 13 as the "Beast," and in 1 John as the "Antichrist."

This notorious personage comes forth in the beginning of the week conquering and to conquer. This does not necessarily mean that he will first break forth on the scene as a mighty military conqueror; this will characterize the latter half of his reign. He probably will conquer and ascend to his dominant position by strategy, intrigue, and flattery. It is stated that when he appears he will overthrow three of the rulers of the ten nations of Revived Rome. He could do this by intrigue and political maneuvering as well as by war. By peace he will destroy many and when they cry "peace and safety, then sudden destruction cometh upon them" (1 Thessalonians 5:3). This unique person will be incarnated by Satan and will receive his power and wisdom from Satan. Through his policy, he will cause craft (industry) to prosper (Daniel 8:25). He will work administrative miracles. The nucleus of this confederation that is already in existence proclaims that the purpose of their confederation is to "cause craft to prosper." They have broken down trade barriers and pooled resources in order to promote this very thing. When the man appears who can work wonders in causing craft to prosper, they will readily accept him. He will probably at first pose as having a humane disposition. It is probably these qualities that cause Israel to make a covenant with him for seven years.

The Second Seal

"And there went out another horse that was red: and power was given to him that sat thereon to take peace from the earth, and that they should kill one another: and there was given unto him a great sword," Revelation 6:4.

When the second seal is broken, this rider comes out on a red horse with a sword in his hand to take peace from the earth. This probably will take place in the middle of the week. This is when the Antichrist places the "abomination of desolation," spoken of by Daniel the prophet, in the holy place. Jesus refers to this abomination of desolation (Matthew 24:15), and also Paul refers to this same incident in 2 Thessalonians 2:3, 4. In Revelation 13, John tells us plainly what this abomination of desolation is. The Roman Church will help consolidate the Beast's empire and is seen in chapter 17 riding the beast as the state church of the ten-nation confederacy. This woman for centuries has had a great affinity for images. The false prophet, the high pontiff of religion in the Beast's empire, will cause an image to be erected to the Antichrist and demand all to worship this image and receive a mark on their foreheads or in their hands. Those who conform seal their doom (Revelation 14:11). Those Christians who refuse will have to die for their salvation. When this image is set up in the holy place is when the covenant with Israel will be broken. Jesus makes it plain that this setting up of the image signals the beginning of the most terrible era the world has ever witnessed. He says, "Neither let him which is in the field return back to take his clothes" (Matthew 24:17, 18). In other words, when this image is set up, the day of slaughter has arrived.

Great have been the wars recorded in the history of the human race, but this will dwarf all of them. Peace will be taken from the earth. It is during this tribulation week that all nations will be gathered against Israel. The kings of the East with their millions will march into Palestine for battle during this week. The Scriptures speak of the merchants of Tarshish participating in a great war at the end of this age (Ezekiel 38:13). Many students of the Scripture believe this refers to England. They also believe "the young lions thereof" refers to the members of the British commonwealth of nations, or the English-speaking peoples, as the lion is an English symbol.

The ingenuity and wealth of the human race are being taxed to produce more horrible weapons of destruction. It is during this war that all these instruments of destruction will be utilized to the limit, including poison gas, hydrogen bombs, and biological weapons.

The Third Seal

"And when he had opened the third seal, I heard the third beast say, Come and see. And I beheld, and lo a black horse; and he that sat on him had a pair of balances in his hand. And I heard a voice in the midst of the four beasts say, A measure of wheat for a penny, and three measures of barley for a penny; and see thou hurt not the oil and the wine," Revelation 6:5, 6.

When the third seal is opened this rider comes out on a black horse with a pair of balances in his hand, measuring out food in a limited amount. This can mean nothing but a famine. Some try to confine the effects of the tribulation to the Beast's empire, but the Scriptures tell us that this tribulation shall come upon all the world, to try them (Revelation 3:10). The center of slaughter as great armies clash will be in Palestine, but the inference is that tribulation, famine, and pestilence will affect the world. Probably, this famine will be caused by so many being at war that the cultivation of the fields will be neglected. It could be caused by biological warfare in which warring nations destroy each oth-

WHEN MEN SEEK DEATH

er's crops, and again it could be caused by God sending adverse weather conditions. It is natural for famine to follow war. Famine ravished many countries after World War I and World War II. Even in our day, after World War II, famine stalked the streets of India and China, and the dead were moved off the streets by being packed like cordwood in trucks.

In Lamentations we get a glimpse of the terrible conditions that will prevail in time of world-wide famine. "Their visage is blacker than a coal; they are not known in the streets: their skin cleaveth to their bones; it is withered, it is become like a stick. They that be slain with the sword are better than they that be slain with hunger: for these pine away, stricken through for want of the fruits of the field. The hands of the pitiful women have sodden their own children: they were their meat in the destruction of the daughter of my people," Lamentations 4:8-10. The above word *sodden* means boiled. Some students of the Scripture think this Scripture is a description of a past famine in Israel's history; even so, whether past or future, this is a good description of conditions under severe famine. It is a historical fact that when Jerusalem was besieged by the Romans during the Maccabean War, the scourge of famine was so great that women agreed to eat each other's children. This famine, soon to come after the Antichrist is revealed, will be more severe than any the world has ever known (Matthew

24:21). With these terrible things in view, Christ warned His people to watch and pray always that they may be accounted worthy to escape these things (Luke 21:36). The way of escape will be the rapture.

The Fourth Seal

"And I looked, and behold a pale horse: and his name that sat on him was Death, and Hell followed with him. And power was given unto them over the fourth part of the earth, to kill with sword, and with hunger, and with death, and with the beast of the earth," Revelation 6:8.

The rider of this pale horse that comes out of the fourth seal is called Death and Hell follows with him. The instruments by which a large part of the human race will be killed are designated as the sword, hunger, death, and the beasts of the earth. These are referred to as the sword, the famine, the noisome beast, and the pestilence in Ezekiel 14:21. They are also called God's four sore judgments. The sword (war) will still be going on and the famine is seen as taking its toll in human lives. The beasts of the forest will be emboldened by starvation until they will slaughter men, and the rigors of the war and malnutrition will weaken men's bodies until disease will sweep over mankind in great epidemics.

The Fifth Seal

"And when he had opened the fifth seal, I saw

under the altar the souls of them that were slain for the Word of God, and for the testimony which they held," Revelation 6:9.

When the fifth seal is opened we get a glimpse of the souls who are martyred by the Beast and the state church for refusing to worship the image of the Beast. In Revelation 13 it is revealed that the false prophet who will be the high pontiff of the state church will make an image to the Beast and all will be demanded to worship the image and receive the mark of the Beast in their foreheads or their right hands. It is a well-known fact the great affinity for images this Scarlet Woman, who will rule in the Beast's empire as the state church, has had down through the ages. This act of sacrilege will reveal who is loyal to the Beast, and those who refuse will be counted traitors and enemies of the Beast's government.

This erection of the image is the "abomination of desolation" referred to by Daniel and Jesus, where they revealed that this act begins the worst part of the great tribulation. Those who worship the image and receive the mark will in reality be worshiping Satan, and the smoke of their torment will ascend up forever and ever (Revelation 14:11). Those who refuse to worship and take the mark will have to die for their stand. Only those who have salvation and fellowship with Jesus will have strength to stand. Those who have salvation and refuse the mark are the ones whose souls are seen under the altar when the fifth seal is broken.

Again it seems possible that the foolish virgins who went to buy oil constitute a portion of these souls under the altar. These souls were conscious; they had their faculties and cried out for judgment against the Beast's government and the state church. A voice tells them to wait just a little season until their brethren shall be killed as they were. It is not long after this when the woman Jezebel of the Dark Ages who has become the Scarlet Woman who rides the Beast will receive her judgment. The kings of the Beast's confederation turn against the state church and burn her flesh with fire (Revelation 17:16). Is it any wonder that Christ warns us to watch and pray that we may be able to escape these things.

The Sixth Seal

"And I beheld when he had opened the sixth seal, and, lo, there was a great earthquake; and the sun became black as sackcloth of hair, and the moon became as blood," Revelation 6:12.

Throughout the prophetical Scriptures it is consistently stated that great physical phenomena will accompany the great tribulation and the second coming of Christ. Here it is stated that there will be a great earthquake, the sun will become black as sackcloth, the moon will become as blood, the stars of heaven will fall, the heavens will be rolled together, and the mountains and islands will be moved out of their places. There have never been physical disturbances such as these since the human race has occupied this earth. In Joel we read about this same event, "And I will show wonders in the heavens and in the earth, blood, and fire, and pillars of smoke. The sun shall be turned into darkness, and the moon into blood, before the great and the terrible day of the Lord come" (Joel 2:30, 31).

Again Isaiah refers to this same time at the end of this age when "all the host of heaven shall be dissolved, and the heavens shall be rolled together as a scroll: and all their host shall fall down, as the leaf falleth off from the vine, and as a falling fig from the fig tree" (Isaiah 34:4). Our Lord foretells these convulsions of heaven and earth and associates them with His second coming. "Immediately after the tribulation of those days shall the sun be darkened, and the moon shall not give her light, and the stars shall fall from heaven, and the powers of the heavens shall be shaken" (Matthew 24:29). This awesome spectacle of God's power will cause those who have rejected salvation, including the great and small of this earth, to cry for the rocks and mountains to fall on them and hide them from the face of God.

The Seventh Seal

"And there came out of the smoke locusts upon the earth: and unto them was given power, as the scorpions of the earth have power. And it was commanded them that they should not hurt the grass of the earth, neither any green thing, neither any tree; but only those men which have not the seal of God in their foreheads," (Revelation 9:3, 4).

Revelation 7 is parenthetical; it portrays the sealing of the 144,000 Jews and a great multitude of gentiles who are saved during the tribulation out of all nations, kindreds, peoples, and tongues. In chapter 8 the seventh seal is broken and out of this seal come the seven trumpet judgments.

These first four trumpet judgments will be terrible, but the last three are so awful that after the fourth trumpet an angel cries with a loud voice, "Woe, woe, woe, to the inhabiters of the earth by reason of the other voices of the trumpet of the three angels, which are yet to sound!"

When the fifth angel sounded his trumpet a star (angel) was seen descending from heaven and opening the bottomless pit. There arose a smoke out of the pit that darkened the sun, and there came locusts out of the pit who were given power to hurt men five months. The locusts will sting the men who have not the seal of God in their foreheads.

These locusts are not ordinary insect locusts, but are wicked spirit beings. The spirit world will be tapped to fill up the horrors of this great tribulation period. These fallen spirits will have bodies like horses, faces like men, hair as the hair of women, and teeth as the teeth of lions. These spirit beings have a king over them, the angel of the bottomless pit. They have tails like scorpions and have stings in their tails. They will torment for five months those men who have not the seal of God in their foreheads.

Nearly 900 years before John saw this vision, God had given Joel a view of this awful army of spirit beings and the havoc they will wreak on men during the great tribulation.

> *"Blow ye the trumpet in Zion, and sound an alarm in my holy mountain: let all the inhabitants of the land tremble: for the day of the Lord cometh, for it is nigh at hand; a day of darkness and of gloominess, a day of clouds and of thick darkness, as the morning spread upon the mountains: a great people and a strong; there hath not been ever the like, neither shall be any more after it, even to the years of many generations. A fire devoureth before them; and behind them a flame burneth: the land is as the garden of Eden before them, and behind them a desolate wilderness; yea, and nothing shall escape them. The appearance of them is as the appearance of horses; and as horsemen, so shall they run. Like the noise of chariots on the tops of mountains shall they leap, like the noise of a flame of fire that devoureth the stubble, as a strong people set*

in battle array. Before their face the people shall be much pained: all faces shall gather blackness. They shall run like mighty men; they shall climb the wall like men of war; and they shall march every one on his ways, and they shall not break their ranks: neither shall one thrust another; they shall walk every one in his path: and when they fall upon the sword, they shall not be wounded. They shall run to and fro in the city; they shall run upon the wall, they shall climb up upon the houses; they shall enter in at the windows like a thief. The earth shall quake before them; the heavens shall tremble: the sun and the moon shall be dark, and the stars shall withdraw their shining," Joel 2:1-10.

It can readily be seen why Christ said there never had been a time like the great tribulation and never will be again.

When the sixth angel sounds, another infernal army of spirit beings numbering 200 million will be turned loose on the human race. These beings are horses with heads as lions and tails as serpents. Fire, smoke, and brimstone will issue from the horses' mouths. The riders of these spirit horses have breastplates of fire, and of jacinth, and brimstone. These terrible spirit beings will slay a third part of men.

When the seventh angel sounded his trumpet,

there were voices in heaven saying, "The kingdoms of this world are become the kingdoms of our Lord, and of his Christ; and he shall reign for ever and ever," (Revelation 11:15). There were also lightnings, and voices, and thunders, and an earthquake, and great hail. We find in Revelation 16:21 that every stone of this hail was about the weight of a talent, which in ancient Hebrew usage was about ninety-three pounds. It is said men will blaspheme God because the plague of this hail is very great. In many of the prophetical Scriptures a great earthquake is associated with the second phase of the second coming of Christ. In Revelation 16:18 we are told that this earthquake will be greater than any earthquake since man has been upon the earth.

The Judgment of the Apostate Church

"And there came one of the seven angels which had the seven vials, and talked with me, saying unto me, Come hither; I will shew unto thee the judgment of the great whore that sitteth upon many waters," Revelation 17:1.

In chapter 16 the angels which have the vials that contain the seven last plagues pour out their vials on the earth; then in the next chapter the judgment of the great whore is revealed. As has been proved previously, this notorious woman is the apostate religions headed up by the Papacy. God promised back in the Dark Ages when this woman was known as

Jezebel that if she did not repent He would cast her into great tribulation. Here is where God executes this judgment. This woman first rides the Beast, or is upheld as the state religion, but near the end of the great tribulation the ten rulers of the confederacy turn against every form of organized religion and burn her flesh as with fire. They probably will be provoked to do this by the rivalry for power between them and the hierarchy of the state church.

The first part of the reign of the Antichrist will be a kind of a triumvirate. The ten rulers will give their power to the beast for a short time. The rulers probably will be induced to do this by the powerful state church. As time progresses, the state church will, as she has done in the past, aspire to supreme power, which will provoke the civil rulers to destroy her. This apostate church is the dominant power now in the early form of this confederacy. Soon after the state church has been destroyed the Antichrist will besiege Israel. This will be the final conflict of the age; all nations will be gathered against Jerusalem (Zechariah 14:2). Even the kings of the East (China, Japan, and others) will be there (Revelation 16:12). At this time the battle of Armageddon will take place. Christ Himself will fight this battle (Zechariah 14:3; Revelation 19:11-15).

The marriage supper will be over and Christ is seen returning to this earth with the glorified resurrected saints. He comes this time as King of Kings and Lord of Lords. He will thrust in His sickle and reap the vine of the earth (Revelation 14:14-16). He is pictured in Isaiah 63:3 as treading the winepress alone. Blood will run in the low places and in ditches to the horses' bridles. Christ will destroy this horde of millions by the brightness of His coming and glory of His power. We find in Zechariah 14:12 that their tongues will consume away in their mouths and their eyes will consume away in their sockets. They will literally melt in His presence. This is the second phase of His second coming when every eye shall see Him and all tribes of the earth shall mourn.

The great tribulation will end with this glorious appearing of the Son of God. When His feet touch the Mount of Olives from whence He departed, the mount will split asunder and fresh water will flow out and heal the Dead Sea (Zechariah 14:8; Ezekiel 47:8-10). The earth shall undergo great physical changes and the long-looked-for kingdom of heaven, a theocracy on earth, will be set up. This will end the great tribulation, the most momentous years earth has ever experienced. A mighty angel will immediately bind Satan and cast him into the bottomless pit and set a seal upon him for one thousand years. This one thousand years will be the Millennial Age when the Davidic covenant will be fulfilled and Jesus Christ will reign here on this earth.

CHAPTER X

THE SECOND COMING OF CHRIST

> *In my Father's house are many mansions: if it were not so, I would have told you. I go to prepare a place for you.*
> *And if I go and prepare a place for you, I will come again, and receive you unto myself; that where I am, there ye may be also.*
> —John 14:2, 3.
>
> *For the Lord himself shall descend from heaven with a shout, with the voice of the archangel, and with the trump of God: and the dead in Christ shall rise first:*
> *Then we which are alive and remain shall be caught up together with them in the clouds, to meet the Lord in the air: and so shall we ever be with the Lord.*
> —I Thessalonians 4:16, 17.

ACCORDING to the Scriptures which never fail, we are facing one of the most glorious, terrible, and momentous events of all time—the second coming of the Son of God. It is saddening to realize how this most glorious hope of the Church has been neglected. Until just recently, one who preached the soon-coming of Christ and the setting up of the kingdom of heaven was looked upon as fanatic by most nominal Christians. Now it is so obvious to sincere students of the Scripture that this great event is near that many of various creeds are preaching the soon-coming of Christ.

The premillennial second coming of Christ is one of the most basic and most emphasized facts in the entire Bible. Although it was unknown to them, the majority of the prophetical utterances of the Old Testament prophets concerning the coming of Christ referred to His second coming. It was unknown to them that there would be two advents and that between the first coming and second coming the mystery of the church age would be fulfilled. They looked forward to the coming that would "restore again the kingdom to Israel." The glowing prophecies in Ezekiel, Daniel, Isaiah, and Zechariah that describe the glory of this kingdom refer to the second coming. All these prophecies make it plain that the kingdom will not be set up until the Messiah comes to reign. Therefore, the doctrine of the postmillennial coming of Christ does not have one Scripture to stand on. The premillennial coming of the Messiah to set up the kingdom of heaven was clearly understood by the Jews in the time of John the Baptist. This is the reason they received John so readily, but rejected the King when He came preaching the mystery form of the kingdom and that to be Christ's disciples one would have to deny himself and take up a cross and follow Him.

The second coming was one of the main tenets of Christ's teaching. He taught them, "If I go and prepare a place for you, I will come again, and receive

THE SECOND COMING OF CHRIST

you unto myself; that where I am, there ye may be also" (John 14:3). He was so definite in teaching His second coming that He gave signs whereby His followers could know when it is near, even at the door (Matthew 24:33). He even taught the second coming in parables. The parable of a man traveling into a far country who after a long time returned and reckoned with his servants is a parable of His second coming, as is also the parable of the ten virgins.

The second coming of Jesus was preached by angels. The angels who spoke to the disciples immediately after the ascension of Jesus said, "Ye men of Galilee, why stand ye gazing up into heaven? this same Jesus, which is taken up from you into heaven, shall so come in like manner as ye have seen him go into heaven" (Acts 1:11). They did not say that Jesus would come at the conversion of a soul or at the death of saints, but this same Jesus would come in "like manner" as they saw Him go into heaven, that is, personally in bodily form and to the same spot, the Mount of Olives (Zechariah 14:4).

The second coming of Jesus is the very heartthrob of the New Testament. It is the glorious hope set forth in the New Testament Epistles as an incentive for Christians to keep the faith and endure persecution. James points to the second coming as the hope for Christians. "Be patient therefore, brethren, unto the coming of the Lord . . . Be ye also patient; stablish your hearts: for the coming of the Lord draweth nigh" (James 5:7, 8). John has warmed the hearts of millions with a throbbing hope as for twenty centuries they have looked from a body wracked with pain, emaciated with disease, or stooped with age, and thrilled at the promise: "When he shall appear, we shall be like him; for we shall see him as he is" (1 John 3:2). Again Paul says, "For our conversation is in heaven; from whence also we look for the Saviour, the Lord Jesus Christ: who shall change our vile body, that it may be fashioned like unto his glorious body, according to the working whereby he is able even to subdue all things unto himself" (Philippians 3:20, 21). Paul encouraged his listeners to look from the troubles of life to the second appearing of Christ when he said, "For the Lord himself shall descend from heaven with a shout, with the voice of the archangel, and with the trump of God: and the dead in Christ shall rise first: then we which are alive and remain shall be caught up together with them in the clouds, to meet the Lord in the air: and so shall we ever be with the Lord" (1 Thessalonians 4:16, 17).

It is not my intention to exhaust the Scriptures that pertain to the second coming of the Son of God; they would be too lengthy. The second coming is one of the most emphasized facts in the Bible. All the glowing descriptions of the kingdom Christ will set up when He comes refer to His second coming. It is time we cease to look on the second coming of Christ as just an article of faith, but as a

THE SECOND COMING OF CHRIST

soul-stirring, world-shaking reality. All the conditions that were to prevail immediately before the second coming of the Lord are here today. It is an utter impossibility for all of these conditions to have just happened simultaneously by accident. The logical question for men to ponder today is, how long will these conditions prevail before the end is ushered in by the second coming of the Son of God?

The world stage is set for the most momentous days in human history. When the wrath of God is soon poured out without mixture and the Antichrist has slain those who fail to take his mark, when the inhabitants of the earth have been decimated by the great tribulation, when man's efforts to rule the world without God have brought utter chaos, when every shred of hope in human hearts has been dashed on the rock of the great tribulation, when every human spirit has been bowed with grief and it seems the human race is doomed; then shall appear the Creator, the same Jesus who came once as a babe to suffer but who now comes as King of Kings to reign.

The second coming will be in two phases. Christ will come as a thief in the night at the first phase of His second coming to resurrect the dead in Christ and to translate the living saints. Paul, referring to this, says, "Behold, I show you a mystery; We shall not all sleep, but we shall all be changed, in a moment, in the twinkling of an eye, at the last trump: for the trumpet shall sound, and the dead shall be raised incorruptible, and we shall be changed" (1 Corinthians 15:51, 52). Christ, referring to this glorious event, says two will be in the bed, one will be taken and the other left; two will be in the field, one will be taken and the other left (Luke 17:34, 36). In other words, it will have an instant effect all over the world. While some are working on one side of the earth others will be sleeping on the other side. The Scriptures make it plain that there will be a taking and a leaving. Those who are ready will be taken, all others will be left.

After this taking away of those who are ready, the marriage supper will take place in the heavens. This glorious time of unspeakable joy and rapture will take place while the terrible tribulation is convening on earth. It is here that the saints will be rewarded for their works. The saints will be given different degrees of rewards and authority in the coming millennial government (Matthew 25:20, 21; 1 Corinthians 15:41, 42). This is because rewards are for the works of a Christian. We will not be rewarded for receiving salvation; this is a free gift by the grace of God. All the saved have eternal life, but all the saved do not have the same reward, because all the saved do not have the same works. "Now he that planteth and he that watereth are one: and every man shall receive his own reward according to his own labour (1 Corinthians 3:8). "And, behold, I come quickly; and my reward is with me, to give every man according as his work shall be" (Revelation 22:12).

After the tribulation and marriage supper are over, the Lord will come with ten thousands of His saints to execute judgment (Jude 14, 15). This is the second phase of the second coming when Christ comes back to earth. This is the time when every eye shall see Him and all tribes of the earth shall mourn (Matthew 24:30). This is when earth has convulsions at the touch of the feet of her Maker. Christ will come to slay the Antichrist's armies which surround Jerusalem. He will cast the Antichrist and the false prophet into the lake of fire and Satan will be bound for one thousand years. At long last, the King is on earth in person and the long-looked-for kingdom of heaven will be set up.

CHAPTER XI

THE MYSTERY KINGDOM

> *From that time Jesus began to preach, and to say, Repent: for the kingdom of heaven is at hand.*—Matthew 4:17.

THE kingdom of God is universal. It encompasses all creation and includes both angels and men (Psalm 103:19). When man was created he was given dominion over the earth, a province of the kingdom of God. When Satan, who had caused rebellion in the kingdom of God in ages past (Isaiah 14), met man on the battlefield of Eden and wrested from man the scepter, he became the prince of this world (John 14:30). He is called the god of this world (2 Corinthians 4:4). He is the author of this world system of government, which is built on force, greed, war, and bloodshed. When he offered these kingdoms to Christ if Christ would worship him, Christ did not deny that in this age they are his. Nevertheless, the earth is the Lord's and the fullness thereof, and in His eternal council He has purposed to bring this world under His complete heavenly rule.

The nation of Israel was created for the purpose

of bearing testimony to the one true God, the King of heaven, and to provide a human lineage for the incarnation of His Son. To David, the divinely chosen king of Israel, God gave the Davidic Covenant which assured David that his throne and kingdom shall be established forever (2 Samuel 7:8-16). God promises that after Israel has been scattered among the nations and the throne vacant for many centuries He will regather Israel from among the nations and restore the kingdom of David (Amos 9:11, 12). Then the angel promises to Mary that Jesus will be given the throne of His father David (Luke 1:31, 33). Commentators do violence to the Scriptures when they try to spiritualize this. David's throne was an earthly throne; therefore, this immutable Davidic Covenant gives earth the assurance that Christ will reign for a certain period of time on a throne on this earth. Christ did not set up this earthly throne at His first advent, but was crucified and gave His life a ransom for many. Therefore, this promised rule of Christ on earth and the fulfillment of the Davidic Covenant is yet future. When God's time arrived, John the Baptist stepped forth and proclaimed the kingdom of heaven to be at hand (Matthew 3:1, 2). Also, Jesus at the beginning of His public ministry proclaimed this kingdom of heaven to be at hand (Matthew 4:17). It was "at hand" because the king, God's Son, was at hand.

"Known unto God are all his works from the beginning of the world" (Acts 15:18). God, knowing

THE MYSTERY KINGDOM

that Israel would not accept the King at His first advent, but rather crucify Him, tells us that fact throughout the Old Testament. Christ, knowing that Israel would not accept Him, foretold the disciples He must be crucified and would rise again the third day. This is why Jesus, when He stood in the synagogue at Nazareth and read from Isaiah 61:1, 2, stopped at the Scripture connected with the first advent and did not read those prophecies pertaining to the second advent. God had promised to send Elijah the prophet before the great and dreadful day of the Lord, which refers to the great tribulation and the second advent. When the disciples brought this Scripture to Christ's attention, He reaffirmed that Elias must first come, but He had already told them in Matthew 11:14 that if they would receive it, John the Baptist was this Elias that was to come. Here we have to go back to the foreknowledge of God. If Israel would have received "it" (the kingdom), Elijah would have had to come; but God, knowing they would reject it, sent John in the spirit and power of Elijah.

In many parables concerning the kingdom of heaven, Christ taught the disciples that before the kingdom in its literal earthly form could be set up, there would be an age in which the kingdom would exist in its mystery phase or spiritual phase (Matthew 13). He taught that by the price of His blood, the medium of faith, and the power of the Holy Ghost, citizens would be naturalized into that kingdom from every tongue, people, and nation, and not from the Jewish nation only (Luke 13:29; Revelation 7:9). Christ began early to try to break through the barrier of their carnal conception of the kingdom of heaven, a conception that the kingdom was only for a favored nation and could be entered only by accident of natural birth (Luke 3:8). Christ taught rather that the time had arrived for man to exercise his God-given power of volition to enter the kingdom and gain eternal life (Revelation 22:17).

Christ further reveals that the way into this kingdom is by a spiritual experience which so affects man morally and spiritually that it is called a new birth and the recipients are new creatures (John 3:3; 2 Corinthians 5:17). The Scriptures teach that these recreated ones who become citizens of the kingdom of heaven are governed by the law of this kingdom which is the perfect law of liberty, or the law of love (James 1:25; 1 Corinthians 13).

Christ taught His disciples to be subjected to the laws of earthly governments which operate under the charter of the Noahic Covenant of human government, unless these laws conflict with the laws of God, which they seldom do in the twentieth century. The laws of human government under the Noahic Covenant give the world some stability and keep down barbarity and utter chaos by providing for the punishment of men by men (Genesis 9:5, 6). The Mosaic law by which God directed the destiny of a nation was a great improvement over the Noahic Covenant because it taught man's moral responsibility to God, the Father of spirits. However, this law was only a schoolmaster to bring us to Christ and His perfect law of liberty (Galatians 3:24). Instead of regenerating man morally until he could be at-one-ment with God, it only showed the great need for a re-creation, and "thou shalt not" met head on with man's carnal desires every day of his life.

The law of liberty is the law of eternity. It is the law of love that governed the universe before Satan brought sin and discord. It governed God's kingdom before any creature had fallen; when the morning stars sang together and the sons of God shouted for joy (Job 38:4-7). It governs the kingdom of heaven (the sphere of God's rule on earth) and will govern all creation in eternity. This law of love, which rules the citizens of the kingdom of heaven, is not something transitory or for a dispensation as the law of Moses was, but is the code for eternity.

In spite of the wide differences in culture, style and personalities of Peter, John, and Paul, they all lift their voices in unison, praising love as the greatest of Christian virtues. Peter lets it top the list of the virtues we are to add to our Christian experience (2 Peter 1:5-7). Paul, the able champion of salvation by faith, places it above faith and hope (1 Corinthians 13:13). Paul goes further and makes the startling statement that one may have faith to remove mountains, or may have the eloquence of angels, or may die as a martyr, but if he is void of love he is nothing (1 Corinthians 13:1-3). He also says it is more excellent than the best gifts (1 Corinthians 12:31). John, in searching for an appropriate term to express the essence of God, said, "God is love." The legislation for the kingdom of heaven is found in the Sermon on the Mount. This is the outward expression of the inward motivation of love shed abroad in the heart by the Holy Ghost. It is neither a high-sounding title nor a conspicuous garb that makes one a citizen of the kingdom of heaven, but it is a new creation and a heart motivated by divine love.

Christ, realizing that the kingdom in its mystery form would break through the confines of national boundaries and include people from every nation, said, "If I be lifted up, I will draw all men unto me." Again He said, "Other sheep I have, which are not of this fold. . . . there shall be one fold, and one shepherd" (John 10:16). No doubt, Christ had in mind souls out in the heathen world such as the centurion, the Ethiopian eunuch, and the Syrophenician woman, who were constitutionally Christians and were ripe for the kingdom of heaven. Before Christ came there had lived out in the heathen world many souls such as Socrates, Plato and Confucius who had been constitutionally Christian and spent their lives yearning for truth. Although they were strangers to the God of Israel and did not have the law of Moses, they were a law unto themselves

THE MYSTERY KINGDOM

(Romans 2:14, 15).

Paul was quick to grasp the truth that salvation by faith was offered to the gentiles and that Christianity was for the whole world. The clash between the particularism of Judaism and the universalism of Christianity, although it vexed Paul, drew from his pen Galatians and Romans, two of the most profound books ever written.

Because the kingdom of heaven in its spiritual phase is referred to in parables as a mystery, many have the erroneous view that it is a mystical allegorical abstraction hard to discern or define. This is unfortunate for those who desire to know God's plan for the ages and where we are in that plan. It is a mystery inasmuch as it was hidden in God from the Old Testament prophets, but in history the kingdom of heaven has been and is now as distinct and tangible a reality as any other historical kingdom. There have been thousands of souls recreated and consecrated by the Spirit and placed into this kingdom where they have served this heavenly King and have lived by His law of love that governs His kingdom. Many have proved their allegiance to this King by giving their lives as martyrs. There are many in the sphere of Christian profession (the net) who are not in the kingdom (Matthew 13:47-50). Yet, there are many who are definitely citizens of the kingdom of heaven, are strangers and pilgrims here and are living in this world, but are not of the world, while they happen to be law-abiding citizens of earthly kingdoms. The kingdom of heaven today is a historical reality. The Priest-king who is on the right hand of God rules over loyal, obedient subjects who are scattered throughout the nations of the world and are anxiously waiting for their King to return and establish His throne on earth. While they wait they are the salt of the earth which keeps the earth from utter moral putrefaction.

CHAPTER XII

THE LITERAL KINGDOM OF HEAVEN

> *And the Lord shall be king over all the earth: in that day shall there be one Lord, and his name one.—Zechariah 14:9.*
>
> *When they therefore were come together, they asked of him, saying, Lord, wilt thou at this time restore again the kingdom of Israel?—Acts 1:6.*

WE FIND the world today divided into two camps, armed to the teeth and poised to fight to the death to determine which of their ideologies shall rule the world: a totalitarian state, or a parliamentarian democracy. Many believe and teach that the two cannot coexist, that one of the two will emerge as victor. God in His omnipotence has foreordained and plainly stated that in the kingdom age earth shall be ruled neither by a totalitarian state nor a parlimentarian democracy, but by a heaven-sent theocracy (Daniel 2:44, 45; Zechariah 14:9).

The fact that the spiritual phase of the kingdom has existed almost 2,000 years and is now nearing its end does not abrogate the immutable promises of God that Christ shall reign on a throne on this earth over an earthly kingdom. It was the present spiritual phase of the kingdom of heaven that was hidden from the Old Testament prophets. Therefore, the facts pertaining to this phase of the kingdom became the mysteries of Jesus' parable. The numerous Scriptures proclaiming a literal kingdom for the Messiah were so plain that they were not mysteries but were understood by all Israel, from the humble shepherd to the scholarly rabbi, from Dan to Beer-sheba. Yet, there are many expositors today who cannot see this kingdom in the Scriptures.

Violence is done to the Scriptures and utter confusion is created when the Scriptures concerning the literal kingdom are applied to the mystery kingdom and vice versa. For instance, Daniel 2:34, 35 where the king from heaven crushes the kingdoms of the world and they become like the chaff of the summer threshingfloor and the wind carries them away and His kingdom consumes all other kingdoms certainly did not happen at His first advent. Also, the prophecy in Isaiah 11 where the wolf shall dwell with the lamb, the lion shall eat straw like the ox and the sucking child shall play on the hole of the asp cannot apply to this age, but is reserved for the future and according to objective analysis of the Scripture, the near future.

When the apostles asked the Lord, "Wilt thou at this time restore again the kingdom to Israel?" they had not yet had their understanding enlightened by the Spirit and had only an elementary understanding of the Scripture. If they had understood the book

THE LITERAL KINGDOM OF HEAVEN

of Daniel, they would have known that the empire that held Israel in subjection at that time (Rome) would have to disintegrate into many separate nations and in the end of the age be revived in the form of a confederacy of nations at the time the kingdom of heaven is set up (Daniel 7:24-27; Revelation 17:13, 14).

If they had understood Ezekiel 37, and scores of other Scriptures, they would have known that there would have to be a dispersion of Israel throughout the nations and then a restoration of the nation before the kingdom of heaven was set up. If they had understood Ezekiel 38 and 39, they would have known that the wild Scythian tribes north of the Caucasus Mountains, who were the descendants of Magog, the second son of Japheth, would have to have time to grow into a mighty military power who could challenge the united nations of revived Rome, and would say of returned Israel, "I will go up to the land of unwalled villages . . . to take a spoil, and to take a prey."

Christ did not think it appropriate to explain all this at this time, so He explained that their immediate task was to build the spiritual kingdom by witnessing to the glorious grace of God that brings salvation to lost men, but He did not teach that this kingdom would not be set up. A few years later when the disciples had been established, strengthened and enlightened by the indwelling Spirit, Christ through that Spirit revealed much more concerning both the mystery and literal phases of the kingdom.

Christ revealed to Paul that blindness in part has happened to Israel until the fullness of the gentiles be come in. Christ revealed to Paul and John that He would not set up the literal kingdom until Satan had had his try at mimicking and thwarting the kingdom of heaven (2 Thessalonians 2:1-4; Revelation 13). He further revealed that Satan would use as his masterpiece the ruler of the confederated nations of revived Rome, who would be the little horn of the Old Testament and the man of sin or the beast of the New Testament (Daniel 7:8; 9:25-27; 2 Thessalonians 2:1-4; Revelation 13).

According to the Scriptures, the world stage is set for the end of this age. The world-shaking event is near when the king will return to gather those who are ready and watching to meet Him in the air. The mystery phase of the kingdom of heaven and the times of the gentiles will end and the glorious millennium of rest will be ushered in.

The literal kingdom of heaven will embrace and bless the whole earth, but Israel will be especially blessed and will be the head of the nations. Israel will again be God's chosen earthly people and her glory will far surpass that of David's and Solomon's time. This will be the glorious time the Hebrew prophets seemingly exhausted themselves trying to describe. The Son of God will reign here on this earth and the knowledge of the Lord will cover the earth as the waters cover the sea (Isaiah 11:9). The old war-ravished earth which has seen multiplied millions of young men torn from the love of their parents and slain on the battlefields will see war no more for one thousand years. In the near future just before this millennium is ushered in, earth will see the greatest carnage in her existence. The blood of millions will run in the ditches to the horses' bridles (Revelation 14:20). During this one thousand years, men will beat their swords into plowshares and their spears into pruninghooks and learn war no more (Isaiah 2:4; Micah 4:3). The instigator of war, Satan, will be bound in the bottomless pit during this one thousand years (Revelation 20:1-3).

The longevity of man that existed before the flood will be restored. "There shall be no more thence an infant of days, nor an old man that hath not filled his days: for the child shall die an hundred years old; but the sinner being an hundred years old shall be accursed," Isaiah 65:20. If a person dies at 100 years of age, he will be called a child. Of course, only the people in their natural bodies will die, the resurrected saints of God who are reigning with Christ will be in their glorified, immortal bodies that cannot die.

During this millennial age, the seasons will be perfect and the earth will produce more bountifully than ever before. "The plowman shall overtake the reaper, and the treader of grapes him that soweth seed," Amos 9:13.

During this kingdom dispensation, the ferocious nature of the animal kingdom will be changed. "The wolf also shall dwell with the lamb, and the leopard shall lie down with the kid; and the calf and the young lion and the fatling together; and a little child shall lead them. And the cow and the bear shall feed; their young ones shall lie down together: and the lion shall eat straw like the ox. And the sucking child shall play on the hole of the asp, and the weaned child shall put his hand on the cockatrice' den. They shall not hurt nor destroy in all my holy mountain: for the earth shall be full of the knowledge of the Lord, as the waters cover the sea," Isaiah 11:6-9. What a strange spectacle shall meet the eye of those who have seen the hatred and cruelty manifested among men and animals in previous ages. There will be no war or enmity among men. The predatory wolf will be seen dwelling with the lamb. The leopard, the kid, the young lion, and the calf shall feed together and a child shall lead them. The ferocious lion, the feared king of beasts, will eat straw instead of meat. The weaned child will play on the den of snakes which were dangerous in past ages. No creature shall hurt or destroy in all the kingdom of heaven.

During this glorious one thousand years, Christ will be King over all the earth and the feast of tabernacles will be observed by all nations. This feast will convene at Jerusalem once a year and if any nation refuses to go to Jerusalem to keep this feast.

THE LITERAL KINGDOM OF HEAVEN 197

they will have no rain until they obey (Zechariah 14:16-19). This war-weary earth that has been drenched with the blood of millions on countless battlefields, this earth that has soaked up the blood of righteous martyrs, this earth that has heard the groans of millions under the cruel hands of tyrants, this earth that has been ravished by disease, war, and famine, shall be soothed and comforted when it is blessed in the near future by the kingdom of heaven.

During this thousand-year reign the remnant of the nations which enter the millennium will increase as the sand of the sea (Revelation 20:8). Contrary to the orthodox belief of a generation ago, men will continue planting and building, buying and selling, and living ordinary lives for one thousand years after Christ's second coming. If the earth burns into a charcoal and men cease to exist in mortal bodies after the return of Christ, as some proclaim, who is it the resurrected saints rule over with a rod of iron? They certainly will not rule each other with a rod of iron. It will be the remnant of the nations which come through the great tribulation and enter into the millennium. The "rod of iron" does not denote cruelty, but supreme authority. At the end of the thousand-year reign, Satan shall be loosed for a little season. He will deceive the nations again and lead them up for his last effort to dethrone God (Revelation 20:1-9). Fire shall fall from heaven and devour their natural bodies and Satan shall be cast into the lake of fire, his eternal doom. It is at the close of the millennium that the white throne judgment takes place and the unsaved dead are judged and cast into the lake of fire. Although long life will be restored during the millennium, yet death will still have power over men. The last enemy Christ shall conquer will be death (1 Corinthians 15:24-28). When death, the last enemy of man, is conquered at the end of the one thousand years, Christ shall deliver the kingdom to God the Father that God may be all in all. Thus time shall end and eternity shall begin. From henceforth through all eternity the throne of Deity will be the throne of God and of the Lamb.

CHAPTER XIII

A NEW HEAVEN AND NEW EARTH

And I saw a new heaven and a new earth: for the first heaven and the first earth were passed away; and there was no more sea.
—Revelation 21:1.

IN PAST generations many preachers interpreted the Scripture in 2 Peter 3:10-12 which tells of the heavens passing away, the elements melting, and the earth and the works therein being burned, as taking place at the second coming of Christ. They made an error of one thousand years. At the end of the millennium is when God will create a new heaven and a new earth. The earth will be burned by fire and every vestige of the curse destroyed. There will be no more sea; therefore, there will be about three times as much land mass as at present. The New Jerusalem, the Lamb's wife, will come down on this renovated earth. God does not reveal much about the wonders of this renovated earth outside the new city. With every vestige of the curse wiped away by fire we may presume that the entire new earth will be as the original Garden of Eden. Some students of Scripture believe the New Jerusalem will hover over our earth during the millennium and the resurrected saints will ascend and descend as the angels did in the vision given to Jacob. The city is called the bride, the Lamb's wife, because it will be the home of the bride. This is the place Jesus said He was going to prepare for the redeemed. What a glorious city! The Creator of the universe is the architect and builder.

The glory of this city is almost unutterable. It is described in Revelation 21 and 22. The length and breadth and height are said to be equal (Revelation 21:16). Its base is a square and it measures 1,500 miles on each side. There is a controversy among students of the Scripture as to the form of this city. It is either a cube or a pyramid. These are the only geometric figures that have the length, breadth and height equal. Some students of Scripture favor the cube form, while others favor the pyramid. If the city is a pyramid, no doubt God's throne will occupy the apex and the city will have four sloping sides over 2,000 miles long. Some reject the idea of the city's being a cube on the basis that if the wall is 144 cubits or 216 feet thick, it could not support itself if it were 1,500 miles high. They reason in terms of natural laws and seem to forget who is the architect and that He hung the earth on nothing. If the city is a cube, it is hard to grasp how one city, with a base on ground level, could reach 1,500 miles high. It is stated that the walls have 12 foundations. It is understood by some that there could be twelve

A NEW HEAVEN AND NEW EARTH

levels of the city or an area equal to twelve cities 1,500 miles on each side with a 6,000-mile perimeter. Whether a cube or pyramid, God has provided a wonderful home for His redeemed. The streets are transparent gold and the foundations of the wall are garnished with twelve varieties of precious stones. The twelve gates of the city are twelve pearls. The city will not be lighted by the sun or the moon, but the glory of God and of the Lamb will lighten it (Revelation 21:23). There will be no temple in the city, for the Lord God Almighty and the Lamb are the temple (Revelation 21:22). The tabernacle of God will be with men and He will dwell with them, "And God shall wipe away all tears from their eyes; and there shall be no more death, neither sorrow, nor crying, neither shall there be any more pain, for the former things are passed away" (Revelation 21:4). Just think of a time when the "former things" will be no more! What are these former things? They are suffering, disease, war, sorrow, tears, toil, and death. In this present evil age it is hard to imagine such a state, but it is God's immutable promise. Redeemed ones can look over this glorious city and never see any mortuaries, funerals, jails, neither suffering nor disappointment. Everyone will be happy, holy, pure, and dwell in immortal bodies fashioned like the resurrected body of the Son of God.

A pure river of water of life shall flow out of the throne of God and of the Lamb and on either side of the river of life shall grow the tree of life which shall bear twelve manner of fruits and yield its fruit every month.

The mansions of this city are not described, but it is enough to know that God built them. They will surpass anything known on this present earth. The greatest accomplishment that can be reached by a human being is to accept God's salvation and make sure that his name is in the Lamb's book of life and that he has a right to one of these mansions.

With this view of the new heaven and new earth, God closes His revelation to man. God has not deemed it appropriate to let mortal man look any farther into the future. Some have even speculated that the universe is too immense for God to be concerned only with this planet. They believe that God in the future will populate other planets or even create new wonders. This is not foretold in His Word. A finite mind can only speculate on the infinite glories to follow. Eye has not seen, ear has not heard, neither has it entered into the heart of man, the things God has in store for those who love Him. All those who understand and know the truth about the nearness of the second coming of Christ should make sure that they know Him and live lives so consecrated that they can pray from the heart, "Thy kingdom come; thy will be done in earth as it is in heaven."

We are now facing momentous days. The night shades of the Great Tribulation can easily be discerned by the diligent student of the Scripture. The